Divine Feminine Energy

Unlocking the Power of the Goddess Within, Connecting with Your Spirit Guides, and Accessing Higher Consciousness through Meditation and Prayer

© Copyright 2024 - All rights reserved.

The content contained within this book may not be reproduced, duplicated, or transmitted without direct written permission from the author or the publisher.

Under no circumstances will any blame or legal responsibility be held against the publisher or author for any damages, reparation, or monetary loss due to the information contained within this book, either directly or indirectly.

Legal Notice:

This book is copyright-protected. It is only for personal use. You cannot amend, distribute, sell, use, quote, or paraphrase any part of the content within this book without the consent of the author or publisher.

Disclaimer Notice:

Please note the information contained within this document is for educational and entertainment purposes only. All efforts have been executed to present accurate, up-to-date, reliable, and complete information. No warranties of any kind are declared or implied. Readers acknowledge that the author is not engaging in the rendering of legal, financial, medical, or professional advice. The content within this book has been derived from various sources. Please consult a licensed professional before attempting any techniques outlined in this book.

By reading this document, the reader agrees that under no circumstances is the author responsible for any losses, direct or indirect, that are incurred as a result of the use of the information contained within this document, including, but not limited to, errors, omissions, or inaccuracies.

Your Free Gift
(only available for a limited time)

Thanks for getting this book! If you want to learn more about various spirituality topics, then join Mari Silva's community and get a free guided meditation MP3 for awakening your third eye. This guided meditation mp3 is designed to open and strengthen ones third eye so you can experience a higher state of consciousness. Simply visit the link below the image to get started.

https://spiritualityspot.com/meditation

Or, Scan the QR code!

Table of Contents

INTRODUCTION 1
CHAPTER 1: WHAT IS THE DIVINE FEMININE? 3
CHAPTER 2: EXPLORING THE DIVINE FEMININE ARCHETYPES........... 16
CHAPTER 3: DISCOVERING THE INNER GODDESS 30
CHAPTER 4: SACRED UNION WITHIN: BALANCING YOUR ENERGIES 42
CHAPTER 5: YOU'RE NEVER ALONE – SPIRIT GUIDES 52
CHAPTER 6: CONNECTING WITH YOUR ALLIES.. 61
CHAPTER 7: CULTIVATING DEEPER BONDS... 69
CHAPTER 8: MEDITATIVE PATHWAYS: ACCESSING HIGHER CONSCIOUSNESS.. 77
CHAPTER 9: PRAYER AS A SACRED RITUAL... 85
CHAPTER 10: A CONTINUAL SPIRAL OF GROWTH................................. 92
CONCLUSION 97
HERE'S ANOTHER BOOK BY MARI SILVA THAT YOU MIGHT LIKE.... 99
YOUR FREE GIFT (ONLY AVAILABLE FOR A LIMITED TIME).............. 100
REFERENCES 101

Introduction

For the longest time, the Divine Feminine has been suppressed. Society has worked ceaselessly night and day to ensure all knowledge of this divine energy is unavailable to anyone. However, times are changing. People are waking up. Most realize they've been sold a bunch of stories by the current establishment – an establishment perhaps desperate to ensure their perverted version of masculinity continues to thrive and suppress others.

No, *this book isn't a war on masculinity*. It's been written to help you understand your life should be full of more ease and flow than it currently is. It will show you how the world could be transformed for the better if it had a balance between creation's dual energies - the Divine Feminine and the Divine Masculine. For far too long, an imbalance has rocked the world on individual and collective levels, causing far more pain and heartbreak than anyone should bear. As you read this book, you'll discover why things are the way they are and what to do.

It all starts with you.

As each person embarks on their personal journey of reconnecting with the Divine Feminine, the world benefits from the snowball effect. More and more people are awakening to the truth of who they are meant to be, including you. You'll experience the benefits of finding a balance between both energies in your personal life and witness the effects of your choices on collective humanity.

There are many benefits to living with an awareness of the power of the Divine Feminine and allowing the Divine Mother's power and love to flow through your life. You may have lived a long time wondering why things aren't working out and questioning whether or not you deserve abundance. The answer to your question is: You absolutely do deserve to live a life full of abundance, bliss, and so much more. You deserve certainty. You deserve the guidance you can depend on, especially when it appears the ground continues to shake and shift beneath your feet.

You deserve the peace of mind that comes with allowing Divine Feminine energy to lead the way and show you a better path to reach your desires. You'll discover how beautiful life can be when you find the sweet spot between the Divine Masculine and the Divine Feminine, channeling in equal portions easily and gracefully.

It is time to stop repressing that which is natural; grace, abundance, peace, prosperity, vitality, and life are your birthright. These and more are qualities that the toxic masculinity of the patriarchy has continued to suppress through heavy-handed methods, like war, violence, deliberate starvation, the calculated continuance of poverty, and the insidious nature of slavery – which is still alive and practiced today.

Unlike other books on the topic, this one is written in simple English, making it easy to understand. Every concept is clearly explained, leaving no room for confusion. The ideas build upon one another sequentially, allowing you to grasp precisely what you need to learn and how to apply your newfound knowledge. You'll appreciate the clarity and practicality of the instructions on these pages. So, if you are ready to discover the power of the Divine Feminine in your life, there's no reason to dilly-dally! Head on to the first chapter.

Chapter 1: What Is the Divine Feminine?

Take a good look at society, and you'll notice an abundance of masculine energy. It doesn't matter what you look at, whether politics, religion, business, or other spheres of life. You'll see the shadow side of masculinity holding swaying human affairs. Now, there's nothing wrong with masculinity or the Divine Masculine energy. However, you need to balance the masculine and feminine energies within you to live a full life. Thankfully, people are becoming more aware of this truth and seeking more information about the Divine Feminine. This energy is awakening within you, and that's why you've chosen this book.

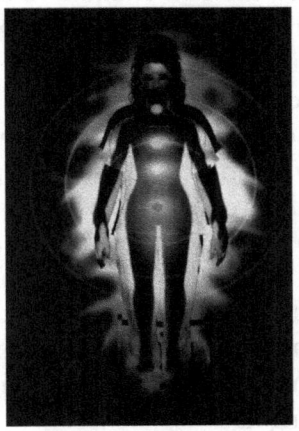

The awakened divine feminine is able to connect with several aspects of her spiritual self.
https://www.pexels.com/photo/light-man-people-woman-6932056/

Before anything else, it's essential to define the Divine Feminine so there are no misunderstandings. The definition is an absolute necessity, especially in light of the present times, with many demonizing anything masculine without understanding that both energies are required in balance.

The Divine Feminine

Everything in life has the Divine Masculine and the Divine Feminine energy within. The same can be said of you. Like many others, you have made do with living in your masculine energy, but it's becoming apparent something's missing from living this way. Through spiritual breadcrumbs, you have been led to this point to discover the true meaning of the Divine Feminine, why this energy is essential, and how you can integrate it into your life to bring balance, ease, and flow to your every waking moment.

The Divine Feminine is a force that has existed since before the dawn of time. It is one half of a whole that is necessary for the creation of all life, known and unknown, still playing a major part in the universe's sustenance. You can think of this energy as the soil. Regardless of what you plant in it, it does not discriminate and will sustain the life of that seed, allowing it to blossom and grow to its fullest potential and continue to nourish it beyond this point. And it's impossible to separate yourself from this energy. Sure, you may not have allowed yourself to flow with it, but it has always been with you.

You can't have the Divine Masculine without the Divine Feminine and vice versa. It has nothing to do with your gender. These energies do not care about how you identify. You may be a man or a woman or identify as something else; still, you have both energies within. When the Divine Masculine is the dominant energy in your life, you come from a place of excess action. You'll have a need to dominate others and exhibit aggressiveness in everything you do and say. You can't understand there are other ways to accomplish your goals that do not require the willingness to cut down others relentlessly. On the flip side, when the Divine Feminine is overly relied upon, you won't make much progress. You lose your power and don't know where to draw the line with yourself or with others. You look at your life, and you get the sense that nothing is moving or changing.

Humans are instinctively drawn toward change and progress. So, when the Divine Feminine does not have the Divine Masculine balancing it out in your life, you feel stuck. The world is one of duality, born from the ultimate reality of unity. The manifestation of the universe is a combination of goddess and god, showing up as woman and man, yang and yin — all of which embody the ultimate forces of the Divine Feminine and the Divine Masculine.

The Qualities of the Divine Feminine

You now recognize the importance of allowing the Divine Feminine energy to flow into and through your life. But how can you tell when you're giving the Divine Mother free rein in your life? These are the qualities of her energy.

- **Intuition.** Split the word into two, and you have "in" and "tuition," teaching that comes from within. It is the knowledge you receive through "illogical" or "irrational" means. It's about knowing things without understanding how. Your intuition is your gut feeling, which, if you follow, leads you to the best results. It warns and keeps you safe from danger or directs you to something you've always desired. Your intuition tells you who's a good person and who isn't. You don't have to wait for them to do something before you know for sure who someone is — not if you follow your intuition's guidance. Choosing to trust your intuition over everything else makes it stronger. Some people have worked on their intuition to the point where they can predict what will happen in the future.

  The more you embody the Divine Feminine, the more intuitive you are. It doesn't matter if you are a woman or a man, as the moment you accept the Divine Feminine influence in your life by embodying it, the more powerful this quality will be. It's no accident that historically, women have always been more intuitive than men. It doesn't mean that men cannot become intuitive. So, if you're a man reading this, know that you, too, can develop your intuition; *don't feel excluded!*

- **Creativity.** The creative process is a feminine one. The most basic form of creativity is childbirth, which only women are naturally equipped to do. Of course, it's impossible to conceive a child without a man playing his part, but childbirth is the woman's ability, seeing as she has a womb in which the child is nurtured before being released into the world when due. Now, what about creativity in every other aspect of life? For some reason, when many think about creativity, they only think about creating movies and cartoons, writing books, singing, acting, dancing, crafts, etc. However, creativity is in every aspect of life. You could be an accountant, but your process still requires creativity.

Using creativity correctly, you can elevate your financial status. Embody the Divine Feminine energy to experience more of its beautiful influence in your life.

You have an energetic body that is made up of energy centers called *chakras*. By unblocking your sacral chakra, you'll experience more creativity in every aspect of your life. This energy center allows the Divine Feminine energy to permeate your existence, and interestingly, it is also the seat of sexual energy required for giving life. There is a connection between sexuality and creativity, both of which are necessary for self-expression. Those who have allowed the Divine Feminine to be more prominent in their lives have no problem with self-expression. They are typically some of the most creative people you'll meet because it is impossible to create without being connected to your intuition and living a life where your heart (rather than your head) drives your choices.

- **Empathy.** The Divine Feminine energy is the fuel for empathy. This basic human trait is much more pronounced in people with the Divine Feminine flowing unimpeded in their lives. Activating or remaining in the Divine Feminine's energy is impossible without being empathetic.

Empathy allows you to connect with your intuition and become a better communicator. Some people think empathy is simply the ability to logically understand what someone else is experiencing. However, it's much more than that. It's about slipping into someone else's shoes and looking at things through their eyes so you genuinely feel their feelings. You embody the sorrow, hurt, anger, joy, ecstasy, or whatever else is in the other's heart.

By deliberately considering what someone else may be going through and how they feel, you encourage the flow of the Divine Feminine. You connect with it better. You find it's not worth judging others because judgment causes toxicity in the connections you share with the people in your life. It's so easy to assume you'd do things differently if you were in the other person's shoes, but the truth is, there's no way to tell whether you would have made different choices in their position.

- **Compassion.** Once you've developed empathy, the next step is to build compassion. These qualities are connected. How? There's no way you could possibly be compassionate if you don't have empathy. Compassion is positive. It causes you to act to alleviate the pain and suffering of those you feel an empathic connection to. The Divine Feminine energy is the urge that drives you toward compassionate actions and choices.

- **Balance.** Where it's more typical of masculine energy to push things to the extreme, the Divine Feminine calls for *balance*. Balance is required in every aspect of your life, whether it's work, love, money, health, etc. Balancing something means finding the sweet spot between two extremes rather than pushing toward one end or the other. It's learning to love others without losing yourself in the process and forgetting you should show yourself love, too. It's being wise about spending your money but not being so frugal that you don't enjoy yourself. It's doing all you can to care for your health by working out, eating right, and getting enough rest without being so extreme that you can't attend to other aspects of your life. It's giving your very best regarding your work, but not so much that you lose yourself, and work becomes your entire identity.

If you observe Mother Nature, you'll realize that balance is in everything. When it rises, the sun doesn't remain pinned to a spot in the sky. It must also *set*. It shines, but not forever, since rain and snow must fall. There is hot and cold, left and right, up and down. The duality of life does not mean you should align yourself with one extreme. The truth about extremes is that they are different sides of the same coin. With the Divine Feminine energy, you'll understand this profoundly and notice your life is balanced as a result.

The Ancient Roots of the Divine Feminine

The Divine Feminine isn't a new concept. Even before there was a term for this energy, it always has been. It's primordial. Comb through history, and you'll find that it's always been honored in some way, as humans realized long ago the sacredness and influence of this force. Even in ancient times, people were aware of the power responsible for creation and fertility, and they represented it using the image of the Great Mother Goddess. Many societies and religions from past epochs highly regarded the Great Mother. Before there was a change in philosophy, this was the norm. The patriarchal religions elbowed their way to the forefront of human consciousness. These religions and philosophies used such brute force in their takeover that they successfully made the Divine Feminine a forgotten concept.

Before the masculine took over, priestesses were more prominent in religious affairs, rituals, etc. Women were revered as the bastions of excellence in the spiritual realm of life's affairs, and there was unmistakable peace in society, unparalleled by whatever has been the most peaceful culture or time under the patriarchy's rule. Things remained blissful until warrior societies slowly but surely grew. Examine ancient societies, religions, and cultures, and you'll find they honored the Mother archetype in the form of Mother Earth, depicting her in various art forms and telling stories and myths about her. That's a far cry from today's reality, with the prominent three religions — Islam, Judaism, and Christianity — being centered on the worship of a masculine God.

Gaia

The ancestors thought of the Earth as the Divine Feminine in physical form, seeing it as a female being that continues to give and sustain life. The way they saw it, the Earth gives life by nurturing plants, which animals depend on. Predators may feast on prey fed by plants. Your ancestors understood that the Mother alone was responsible for the relentless flow of life and that when plants and animals die, they return to her only to be born again. In other words, the Divine Feminine is about the cycle of birth, death, and rebirth. There would be no ecosystem without Mother Earth. She is the ultimate life-giver, nurturer, and healer. Creation and destruction are in her hands, both essential to life's continuation. But where, precisely, was the idea of the Earth as a mother first documented? The first reference to this idea is in the writings of the ancient Greeks, who referred to the Divine Feminine as

Gaia, the mother of creation and the Earth goddess, in the 7th century BCE. According to the Greeks, all life began with only three Divine beings: Chaos, Gaia, and Eros, with Gaia being the mother of every Divine being.

Venus of Willendorf

Sculpture of Venus of Willendorf, one of the oldest representations of the Divine Feminine.
*Jakub Hałun, CC BY-SA 4.0 <https://creativecommons.org/licenses/by-sa/4.0>, via Wikimedia Commons
https://commons.wikimedia.org/wiki/File:Venus_of_Willendorf,_20210730_1214_1255.jpg*

Head over to Austria, and you'll find one of the oldest representations of the Divine Feminine in Willendorf, Venus of Willendorf. Historians believe she was crafted between 25,000 and 20,000 BCE, back in the Paleolithic epoch. The sculpture may be small, being only 4.3 inches in height, but her significance to the people stands immeasurably far above and beyond that height! The figure has no face. She has an overhanging stomach, acting as a roof over her prominent pubic region. Above her belly are large breasts. Together, these features represent life, pregnancy, birth, and fertility. This sculpture is faceless to shift the focus to her body, which signifies everything about life and the sustenance thereof. Interestingly, there aren't as many masculine figurines from the Paleolithic times as there are feminine ones, clarifying that the society of the time was matriarchal.

The Sleeping Lady of Malta

The Sleeping Lady of Malta.
Hamelin de Guettelet, CC BY-SA 3.0 <https://creativecommons.org/licenses/by-sa/3.0>, via Wikimedia Commons https://commons.wikimedia.org/wiki/File:Sleeping_Lady_Hal_Saflieni.jpg

The Sleeping Lady is another illustration of the Divine Mother in a Neolithic burial ground in Malta. Its precise location is the Gal Saflieni Hypogeum, now a UNESCO World Heritage Site. She's depicted as a woman with curves, fast asleep on a bed, lying on her side. Historians and scholars believe she's connected with the eternal sleep of death because the figure was discovered at a burial site. She was seen as the Goddess of Regeneration, reigning supreme over the processes of birth, death, and rebirth. It's also hypothesized that she was revered at a time when people were transitioning from hunting and gathering to farming, cultivating their crops, enabling them to remain in one spot rather than live a nomadic life. This switch in lifestyle came with its attendant issues, which would've put an end to their livelihood if they hadn't addressed it. So, it was natural that they turned toward the Divine Feminine, who they knew could help them with cultivation and procreation.

The Cycladic Female Figurines

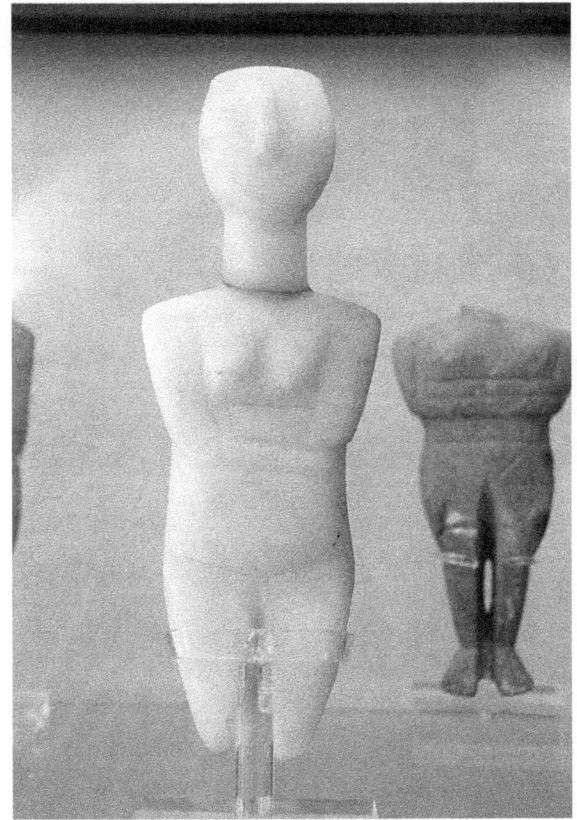

The Cycladic female figurine.
Zde, CC BY-SA 3.0 <https://creativecommons.org/licenses/by-sa/3.0>, via Wikimedia Commons: https://commons.wikimedia.org/wiki/File:Cycladic_female_figurine_2800-2300_BC,_AM_Naxos,_143160.jpg

The Cycladic female depiction of the Divine Mother differs from the previously mentioned goddesses, as she isn't voluptuous. Looking at her belly, you can see a gentle swell indicating pregnancy. This figure has her hands folded beneath her breasts, a pose reminiscent of other images from Cyprus, Palestine, Syria, and other Eastern Mediterranean regions. In those times, people died much more often and younger than presently. Because of this high mortality rate, the people sought the favor of the Mother Goddess through these statuettes, asking her to protect and keep them safe.

The Snake Goddess of Crete

The Snake Goddess of Crete.
https://commons.wikimedia.org/wiki/File:Simplified-stylized_Minoan_snake_goddess_symbol.svg

    The Snake Goddess from the Knossos palace is from circa 1600 BCE. This portrayal of the Goddess was revered by the people of Crete, specifically those in the ancient Minoan Civilization. She's different from the previous iterations of Mother God because her design is much more intricate. Her sensuality is undeniable, as she's dressed in a fancy skirt with her breasts bare, both symbolizing the nourishment of breast milk, fertility, and the sexuality of the feminine. She has a snake in each hand, and for good reason, since snakes are connected to the underworld, regeneration, and healing. The Minoans held women in high regard in societal and religious matters, and their life was built on an impressively organized system where agriculture was efficiently handled.

Maat

Maat was the embodiment of justice, balance, and truth.
Eternal Space, CC BY-SA 4.0 <https://creativecommons.org/licenses/by-sa/4.0>, via Wikimedia Commons: https://commons.wikimedia.org/wiki/File:Maat_(Goddess).png

Ancient Egyptians had a plethora of female goddesses. These expressions of the Divine Feminine were the bastions of order, morality, conception, fertility, values, etc. Maat was about maintaining the harmony of the cosmos. She was the embodiment of justice, balance, and truth. Maat's followers believed that when they passed on, the weight of their hearts would be measured against that of the ostrich feather she wore on her head. Those whose hearts were as light as Maat's feather could pass over to paradise, ruled by Osiris.

Why Should You Connect with the Divine Feminine?

You don't need to subscribe to certain religious beliefs to benefit from the Divine Feminine energy flowing into your life. It is helpful to know because you can begin to transform your life right now. You should want the touch of the Divine Mother in your life for the following reasons:

1. You'll experience increased intuition, which will steer you where you want to go and away from danger or anything that doesn't serve you.
2. You'll become a more compassionate person, which opens you up to experiencing compassion and care from others, too.
3. You'll learn to relax and trust life more. It's a necessary gift in a world designed to give you more reasons to be anxious and insecure each day. The Divine Feminine will teach you how to relax and receive and manifest your dreams by energetically aligning with your desires rather than using brute force.
4. You'll be more in tune with life, which will help your creativity.
5. Your awareness and allowance of Divine Feminine energy will lead you to find a balance between the feminine and the masculine. As a result, you'll be in a much more powerful position than others, equipped to change your life as needed because you have the direct action of the Divine Masculine and the intuitive guidance and magnetism of the Divine Feminine.

By exploring and interacting with the Mother energy, you'll develop an intuitive comprehension of spiritual matters. Why does that matter? It's because everything in life comes from spirit, so if you can crack the code by finding the balance between both polarities, you'll have a life you love more and more each day.

Once more, nothing about the Divine Feminine or Divine Masculine has to do with gender, so it's best not to tie it to simplistic affairs, which are of no consequence in the ultimate reality of life. That would be reductive. Spirit isn't about those things. While many combat the idea of the Divine Feminine by arguing it's feminism wearing a new mask, they're absolutely incorrect. Also, the Divine Feminine isn't an excuse for people to push their borderline fanatical ideologies whether or not multiple genders or "being non-binary" is valid — *never mind that "non-binary" automatically creates a binary!*

Some people have attempted to weaponize the Divine Feminine by labeling it an attack on their religion or an attempt to encourage a female answer to the red pill movement that's just as toxic. Once more, the Divine Feminine and Divine Masculine are not about these spiritually immature debates. Knowledge of this energy has to be spread to allow the integration of both halves, which exist in every person and everything. This integration will create the possibility for a much more harmonious life than what humans have had to contend with in recent history.

If everyone were to learn to find the balance between these divine polarities, they would quickly realize how moot certain debates and conversations are. Humans are much more than their sexualities, genders, or how they identify. You, too, will be empowered by understanding the truth about the Divine Feminine. You can connect with the Goddess within and see for yourself how your life changes exponentially for the better.

Prompts to Connect with the Divine Feminine

1. Can you recall a moment in life or a dream where you felt the nature of the Divine Feminine energy powerfully, expressed through creativity, intuition, nurturing, or any other of its qualities?
2. Based on the qualities of the Divine Feminine explained earlier in this chapter, could you think of three ways to promote the flow of the Divine Feminine energy each day?

Chapter 2: Exploring the Divine Feminine Archetypes

Before exploring the different Divine Feminine archetypes, you need a proper understanding of what archetypes are. Swiss psychiatrist Carl Jung is the brilliant mind who developed the concept of archetypes in the 20th century. But that doesn't mean these archetypes didn't exist before he identified and named them. They are intended to show you that femininity has multiple facets. Archetypes are patterns of behavior and expression that exist in everyone.

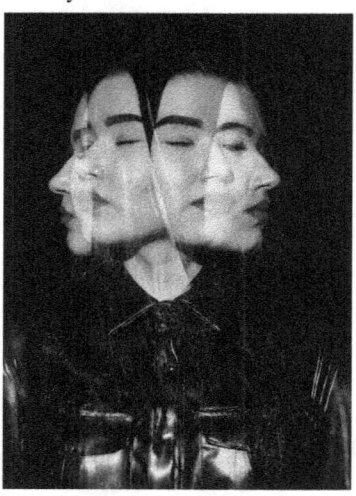

Femininity has multiple facets.

https://www.pexels.com/photo/a-multiple-exposure-photography-of-a-woman-in-black-leather-top-7676532/

The female archetypes are the embodiments of various characteristics and experiences that are unique to femininity. Does this imply there are only as many kinds of women as there are feminine archetypes?

No.

For one thing, the female archetypes apply to everyone, female and male. For another, the idea of archetypes isn't meant to put people into neatly labeled boxes but to offer various perspectives on how feminine qualities are embodied and expressed.

Are these archetypes only negative or positive? They have their light and shadow aspects. Life is complex, and so are people. It's unrealistic to think that any idea, thing, or person is all light or all darkness, all good or all bad. This black-and-white thinking only serves to inhibit true understanding of spirituality and, by extension, life. Another thing to keep in mind as you delve into archetypes is that they're not death sentences, static and unchanging.

It is possible to experience different archetypes at the same time or to switch from one to another. Your archetype may depend on what phase of life you're in. Also, you may change archetypes, embodying one at home and a different one at work and yet another regarding health, finances, etc.

With your understanding of feminine archetypes, you'll know what drives you, how you handle your relationships, and what choices you'll likely settle on. You'll understand how you navigate life and why others respond to you as they do.

The Four Main Feminine Archetypes

The main female archetypes are the **Maiden, Mother, Wild Woman, and Crone**. You can think of them as spiritual or energetic blueprints you can plug into. It's best to honor each of these in your life because you'll fail if you choose to suppress them. Even worse, you'll call forth the dark aspect of this archetype in your life, the shadow side. The result? You'll experience psychological problems like depression and anxiety, with your life feeling wildly out of balance. Your relationships and physical health will break down as you attempt to suppress these aspects of yourself. Therefore, you have to know them and learn to love them.

1. The Maiden

Light Aspects: Openness, potential, innocence, adaptability, new beginnings, purity, playfulness, receptivity, and curiosity.

Shadow Aspects: A refusal to release childhood indecisiveness, self-doubt, resistance to growth, fear, escapism, stagnation, naivety.

Spiritual Correspondences: Intuition, water, springtime, the moon, new beginnings, sunrise.

Goddesses: Osun, Aset, Asase Yaa, Hestia, Artemis, Amaterasu, Guanyin, Rhiannon.

The maiden.
https://pixabay.com/photos/woman-scandinavian-young-face-7708174/

About This Archetype: The Maiden is the embodiment of purity. The common misconception is that "maidenhood" in this context refers to sexuality, but really, it's a state of mind. It's about a state of autonomy and independence, where you refuse to allow anyone or anything a pedestal in your life. You're your own person. The energy of the Maiden is strong, dynamic, full of youth and joie de vivre. When you allow this energy to flow, you're magnetic to the good things in life. You're full of positivity, keeping your mind and heart open to the new, unafraid of throwing yourself wholeheartedly into unfamiliar realms, excitedly asking, "What if?"

The Maiden has no responsibilities weighing her down and no negativity or doubt from past experiences. When you embody this energy, you're assertive, unafraid to plan, and willing to connect with others as you're at your most sociable. You know there's much to discover about yourself and life, and you embrace every chance to learn. You take care of yourself, taking the time to dress well and strengthen your body through exercise.

2. The Mother

Light Aspects: Protection, fertility, creativity, care, compassion, selflessness, nurturing, empathy, and abundance.

Shadow Aspects: Smothering, martyrdom, sacrifice, control, neglect of self, resistance to change, overprotectiveness, and a desperate clinging to the past.

Spiritual Correspondences: Summer, stability, full moon, groundedness, Earth.

Goddesses: Isis, Kali, Demeter (Ceres), Gaia, Terra Mater, Cybele, Maia, Nammu.

The mother.
https://pixabay.com/photos/pregnant-woman-belly-mother-parent-6178270/

About This Archetype: The Mother archetype is the embodiment of fertility. She is sensuous in all her ways, never lacking for anything since she is abundance itself. As the Mother, your compassion knows no bounds, and neither does your generosity. You're also at your most creative, supportive, caring, and nurturing. The Mother isn't one to spoil senselessly, as her love is sweet, soft, yet tough. Across religions, cultures, and myths, the Mother is the Earth herself. She is the one true body upon which the flora and fauna of life "live and move and have their being."

When you express your inner Mother, you slow down and focus on being present, understanding that the here and now is the ultimate gift life offers. You're full of gratitude for where you are and willing to share this with the people you appreciate in your life. Even your clothing reflects this energy, as you favor more comfortable clothing that doesn't hug too tightly or restrict your movement. If you want to amplify this energy more, you'd be hard-pressed to find a better way than spending time in nature. As the Mother, you care for yourself, shelving everything you allow to become more important than living and realizing there's no business or job more important than living and being human. You get in touch with your heart, only doing what feels right as you realize it's the only obligation you have.

3. The Wild Woman

Light Aspects: Transformation, potential, courage, freedom, resilience, wisdom, self-expression, passion, creativity.

Shadow Aspects: Volatile emotions, aggression, jealousy, self-sabotage, recklessness, possessiveness of fear of commitment, destructiveness.

Spiritual Correspondences: Fire, energy, passion, autumn, wild places, the solar plexus, the South.

Goddesses: Sekhmet, Bastet, Kali, Diana, Lilith, Frey, the Morrigan.

The wild woman.
https://pixabay.com/photos/pink-hair-hairstyle-woman-makeup-1450045/

About This Archetype: The Wild Woman archetype is darker than the previous two, and for some reason, many misunderstand this archetype. They don't realize this archetype is a healer in her own right. Consider the image of a medicine woman, in touch with nature, knowing its secrets, and refusing to be tamed or "cultured." This archetype signifies the soul waking up to the true, ultimate reality of life after a long time of being fast asleep, lulled into a comatose state by the lies and illusions of physical life. She is the Wild Woman only because she defies logic, being greater than it, tapping into the realms of the magical, which society neither takes seriously nor makes room for.

Thanks to the Wild Woman, you have full access to your inner knowing, remaining permanently connected to your intuition. It's this archetype that carries healing power. There's nothing rational about her ways. She is a terror to those who cling desperately to the need to make sense of things. The human mind fears what it doesn't understand and cannot predict. The Wild Woman will remain unknown to the mind that hasn't accepted that there are things too great to be contained by the step-by-step sequence characteristic of logical, rational thought.

The patriarchal system of doing things has worked ceaselessly to erase everything about the Wild Woman, silencing those who dare to speak up about this archetype or express it. However, she's very present, and you can connect with her. The reason she is so suppressed isn't that she's problematic but because society's ills and restrictions would crumble were she allowed full expression, and some would hate for that to happen. You may have become a willing participant in her suppression, not allowing her to express herself in your life. The previous statement isn't to shame you but to help you break free from the sleepy spell cast on you through educational and media conditioning.

You need to step back from connecting with others and withdraw within to embody the Wild Woman. Also, you shouldn't give your power or attention away to screens. Instead, connect with yourself through mindful practices like meditation. The Wild Woman has boundaries she fiercely protects, saying no to anything she doesn't want without remorse. She enjoys nature, expresses her rage, and doesn't shy away from shadow work to reveal her darker aspects and integrate them.

4. The Crone

Light Aspects: Acceptance, death and rebirth, mystery, release, insight, transformation, guidance, and wisdom.

Shadow Aspects: Isolation, cynicism, an excessive desire to control, a desperate clinging to the past, cynicism, bitterness, fear of death, and a deep resistance to change.

Spiritual Correspondences: Winter, twilight, dark moon, endings and beginnings, the void.

Goddesses: Cailleach, Baba Yaga, Cybele, Hecate, and Las Cacareas (The Old Cacklers).

The crone.
https://pixabay.com/photos/old-woman-veiled-woman-veil-turkey-4189578/

About This Archetype: She's known as the Wise Woman and isn't accorded the respect she deserves. People only think of this archetype as old, infertile, and inactive. They think of her as the loss of beauty, but that's not what this archetype is about. In popular culture, she is shown as a wicked witch, an old woman cast out from society, banished to the furthermost reaches of the community. She's described as bitter with a chip on her shoulder, willing to destroy with trickery.

However, there's a power to her that many are unaware of. Her slowness embodies mystery, which stands in contrast to the fast-paced life many are used to. Her life is rich and full of wisdom and meaning. She is in a position where she isn't required to achieve anything, nor does the allure of "productivity" seduce her. She is free from all expectations, putting her in the singular position of having nothing to lose. That is the actual reason she's villainized. The person with nothing to lose has true freedom, and it is a power that can bring even the greatest to their knees.

The Other Feminine Archetypes

The Warrior

The Warrior archetype is about justice. She's not afraid to fight. When you embody this archetype, you find it difficult to condone wrongdoing, say nothing, and act like it didn't happen. You're not a person who will mince words. You're unafraid to tell it exactly as it is. You do more than speak up; you act to correct injustice when you can. Whenever you cannot help others, you'll rally every resource and person you can to assist you.

As the Warrior, you don't care about your personal safety because you are committed to the mission of setting things right. Think of yourself as a mother bear, fiercely protecting her young to death. That's what it means to embody this archetype. You couldn't care less about whether or not you make enemies as long as you restore justice and balance. You aren't concerned about being inconvenienced or having your comfort taken from you as long as you ensure justice prevails.

Being a Warrior means you are a physical person. Your mind and body possess stamina, strength, and resilience beyond compare. You're an inspiration to others around you. You know how to transmute the energies of rage and anger and channel them toward productive ends. Women in history who have embodied this archetype include Rosa Parks and Joan of Arc.

The Enchantress

The Enchantress archetype is about mystery. Her function is seduction. In this energy, you are more open to the unknown, daring to leave your comfort zone for the wild world beyond what you understand. As the Enchantress, you are no longer tethered to your past because you refuse to be defined by it. Instead, you are magnetized toward the future, drawn by the siren call of your dreams and the possibility of what could be. The Enchantress's aura is magnetic, drawing everyone in. She sweetly helps you realize your truest desires and dares you to pursue them. Why? She wants you to see how much more magical your life could become if you left the comfort of the familiar.

Jacqueline Kennedy is a historical enchantress.
https://commons.wikimedia.org/wiki/File:Jacqueline_Kennedy_in_Venezuela_crop.jpg

The Enchantress is charismatic, and barely a soul can withstand her charm. You are confident when you embody this archetype, and it's hard not to see that. You're a bold, brilliant light, so bright that you force others to do a double-take whenever you walk into the room. The world is your stage. You are the leading lady; everyone else is a supporting actor or extra — but you are not an obnoxious leading lady! You're a mirror for others, showing them how much more they could be. Those who are too insecure to withstand the brightness of your light have no choice but to turn away or get out of your way because you have no intention of dimming your glory for their comfort. Historical enchantresses include Mata Hari, Cleopatra, Eva Peron, Jacqueline Kennedy, and Madame de Pompadour.

The Lover

Playing out this archetype makes you passionate and on fire for life. A sensual person, nothing escapes your notice. You pick up on everything from textures to smells, colors to sounds, etc. You're a person who understands the value of being present, ever rooted in the here and now. You realize that life is romance — not in the shallow way depicted in books and movies, but in how you approach everything with a lover's heart.

As present as you are, you recognize that the past has valuable treasures. When life becomes too dark and burdens too heavy to bear, you look for the good in your situation. The love you carry in your heart that helps you relentlessly press forward, unafraid and willing to drop your ego with reckless abandon. As the Lover, you're aware of your worth. You know that you have unquestionable value. Therefore, nothing is too good for you.

You recognize that you deserve the best in life and understand that others do, too. No one is more aware of the fleeting nature of life than you are, so you savor every sweet drop of life's nectar and offer yourself in full in return. You're aware that your love puts you in a vulnerable position where you could be hurt, but you understand it's par for the course. It's not enough to make you withdraw or retreat. If you'd like to understand this archetype better, you should read Rumi's works.

The Healer

The Healer archetype considers everything to be whole. Others may see brokenness and imperfection, but that's not how she views the world. Her heart is sensitive and bleeds for others, unable to look upon people who are suffering without feeling empathy and compassion. Similar to the Warrior archetype, the Healer archetype does not rest in the face of pain and suffering. However, her approach is gentler.

When you are the Healer, you take care of others *and yourself* because you understand that you cannot give what you don't have. You know the intricate connection between body, mind, and spirit and that all three aspects of self must be nurtured and tended to. The Healer naturally knows what would help every situation. The body and the Earth have wisdom beyond compare, and as the Healer, you have the intuitive ability to connect with this wisdom. So, you know what would work as a solution or a healing medicine at any point in time, regardless of the ailment. You will embody this energy more with a mindfulness practice like meditation. Mother Teresa would have been a great example of the Healer archetype, but she gave in to her dark side and expressed it toxically.

The Visionary

The Visionary is also called the *Prophet* or the *Seer*. Traditionally, the people who embody this archetype are known for predicting the future. There's more to this archetype than envisioning possibilities. She takes action, channeling her energy toward inspiring herself and others to move toward what could be. One of the most fascinating things about The Visionary is the power that lies within her voice. She has a way with words that draws hearts and minds toward her message. She understands the power of the spoken word and how it can move people toward healing or destruction.

Many people fear the unknown, refusing to try something new because it's never been done before. However, this archetype couldn't care less about whether or not a thing has ever been done. She's far more interested in potential, which lies beyond the realms of the familiar and the known. She transmutes the energy of fear into courage and faith. With these traits, she rides into new territories and conquers them for the benefit of everyone. Famous oracles include Cassandra of Troy, Deborah the Prophet, Miriam (Moses's sister), and the Delphi Oracle Sybil.

The Creator

The Creator desires to express life and beauty in every way possible. She can craft worlds yet unimagined by any mind and bring them to pass. Where others see what eyes will allow them to see, the Creator sees beyond what is. Not only that, but she can also bring what she sees into physical reality. If you embody the Creator archetype, you understand you're not doing the creation yourself. Instead, you're serving as a channel or a conduit to allow creativity to flow through you and take whatever form it will, whether it's a pair of socks you're knitting or a piece of music you're composing. The Creator is most fulfilled when she can create. If you've been feeling depressed or out of touch with life, you may find it helpful to tap into this side of yourself. Excellent examples of this archetype include Jane Austen, Virginia Woolf, Augusta Savage, Louise Bourgeois, and Sapho.

An example of the creator archetype is Virginia Woolf.
https://commons.wikimedia.org/wiki/File:George_Charles_Beresford_-_Virginia_Woolf_in_1902.jpg

The Queen

This archetype is all about building a legacy. Every archetype is capable of being a leader. However, the Queen is a natural at this. You should know that of all the archetypes, she is the most masculine-leaning. When you are the embodiment of the Queen, you understand how powerful it is to approach every problem using strategy, and you realize that your goal is to serve a purpose higher than your personal ambitions. Your decisions aren't selfish, as you settle upon them only after thorough consideration of everyone and everything that will be affected. You realize the importance of considering the consequences. While you recognize the allure of living life on your own terms, you choose to sacrifice it in pursuit of goals beyond the ordinary. By doing this, you plunge your life into meaningful depths far beyond what others could possibly fathom.

Like the Warrior, you have unparalleled energy. You don't allow anything to take your focus away from your highest calling and purpose. While you're always paying attention to various perspectives and opinions on what would be the best course of action, you alone are the final arbiter who determines what should happen. When you make your pronouncements, they're not up for negotiation or discussion. Everyone must fall in line with your decree. Individuals who exhibited the true Queen energy include Margaret Thatcher, Queen Elizabeth I, Queen Elizabeth II, and Queen Victoria; Athena, the Greek goddess of martial strategy and wisdom; Pharaoh Hapshetsut; and Pharaoh Nefertiti.

The Priestess

Nothing matters more to the Priestess archetype than enlightenment. Being a mystic, she desires to see the connection between all things physical and spiritual. As a priestess, you do not condemn anything as being profane because you realize that all things spring from one source and, therefore, are sacred. You have the critical role of reminding people of their divine origins and calling them back to their true selves. As the Healer and Warrior do, you desire nothing more than to bring things back to their proper order. However, you fight this battle on the spiritual, energetic plane.

You bring people back to the truth of who they are by transmuting darkness into light. You've spent time in isolation, studying the ways of spirit and how it expresses itself in the physical world. Intuitively aware of the old ways and knowing how to use them, you create a life that works for all. Others may think of miracles as one-offs, things that only happen now and then. But for you, miracles are moment-to-moment things. Where people see nothing but a dead end, you see a way through every time.

You know you could never be stuck because you're never alone. You carry within the divine power of the ultimate source of all things. This is the power of God. You recognize that even though things seem random and chaotic, they are according to a divine script that cannot be altered and ultimately leads to the enlightenment of everyone. You take the verse, "Ask, and you shall be given; seek, and you shall find; knock, and it shall be opened unto you," quite literally — not because you're delusional, but because that has been your life experience. Examples of people who have embodied this energy include Rabiah al-Adawiyya al-Qaysyya, Lalleshwari, Hildegard of Bingen, Therese of Lisieux, Mirabai,

Alexandra David-Neel, and Hazrat Babajan.

What's Your Archetype?

Having read through all these archetypes, you may find yourself a bit confused because you recognize yourself in each one. It almost makes you assume that the whole concept of archetypes must be nonsense, doesn't it? There's no such thing as having one particular archetype. You can fluidly move from one to another or embody several at the same time. However, you may have noticed that you approach life through the lens of a specific archetype more than the others.

This awareness will help you navigate your existence much better than you've been doing. Why? You'll find a way to balance all these archetypes, moving fluidly from one to another as needed, because every situation in life requires different strategies and tactics to approach them. When you can recognize your dominant feminine archetypes and integrate them, you transform your life for the better. Before heading on to the next chapter, here are questions to reflect on to understand your inner world better:

1. Of all the archetypes presented, which feels closest to your aspirations and experiences?
2. As you ponder individual aspects of your life (spiritual, mental, physical, and emotional), which archetypes do you embody the most in each one?
3. Which archetype were you the least connected to? Why do you think that is?
4. Which archetypes do you wish you could embody but feel like you can't? Why?

The chapters to come will help you discover who you are and connect you to your unique expressions of the Divine Feminine energy, particularly regarding the four major feminine archetypes.

Chapter 3: Discovering the Inner Goddess

Your inner goddess is nothing like the mask you've had to put on to get through daily life. Her authentic self resides within you, and her power and confidence are beyond compare. She doesn't care about what society expects from you, and she has neither the time nor the patience for self-doubt. You honor your true self when you allow her to manifest in your life. Your strengths shine through, and you no longer hide your passions for fear of being put down or mocked. You don't care because you know there's nothing more fulfilling than being your true self. She is that part of you that helps you be inspired to create and will encourage you through the darkest and worst of times.

Unleash the goddess within.
https://easy-peasy.ai/ai-image-generator/images/stimulate-ajna-visualize-vibrant-indigo-lotus-flower-spiritual-awakening

The Benefits of Connecting with Your Inner Goddess

Everyone wants to experience personal growth and be their best, but not everyone knows how. Well, there's no better way to accomplish this goal than by getting in touch with the Divine goddess within you. As you do, you'll exhibit wisdom, power, and grace in all that you do, as you're no longer pulled this way or that by voices and circumstances around you. The goddess's tuition within leads you. There's nothing better because she knows what you need to thrive better than anyone else, and relying on her guidance will give you confidence in yourself.

Have you felt disconnected from life? Do you get the sense that you're not living out your purpose? Do you feel like your life has no direction? If so, you'll find many benefits from getting in touch with your inner goddess. As you do, you'll finally be able to look at everything in your life with acceptance.

Even the things you once criticized yourself terribly for will take on a new sheen, and you'll see there's not one part of who you are that doesn't deserve your love. You'll find how all your traits come together to make you who you are, someone irreplaceable. Every archetype has its light and dark side, and so does every human. When you accept this truth, you accept yourself, and you stop laboring under the burden of unfair comparisons. You put away the childish business of setting unrealistic expectations for yourself, and as a result, your self-esteem will be restored.

Another benefit of embracing your inner Goddess is you'll drop all the masks and costumes you've worn your entire life. You picked them up only as a matter of survival because you'd learned from an early point in life that the world wouldn't accept you if you showed up as your true self. However, these costumes and masks have done nothing more than dim your light. They've made you forfeit the radiance of your true, authentic self, shunning it and choosing the tattered rags of compliance and society's definition of acceptance, which, at its core, is fake. Society's acceptance is a message to your soul that you will be welcomed with open arms as long as you show up as anyone but who you are. That's not acceptance. That's a proposition forcing you to reject yourself, and it's so insidious because you remain unaware that no one has the power to reject you but you.

None of this is your fault, so don't waste time wallowing in self-blame. Now that you're aware of how the wool has been pulled over your eyes, you can fix the problem with the help of the Divine Goddess within you. Her light will cut through the darkness of inauthenticity if you allow it, and you'll remember how to breathe once more for the first time in a long time. You'll remember what makes you tick, what makes you smile, what fuels you with joy and life, and you'll go after these things with the relentless tenacity of a thousand shire horses, just as you did when you were a child before the world got into your head and told you who you were was unacceptable.

As you embody your authentic self, you draw a community of others close to you who share the same vision. You pull in people who have done away with the need to mask or pretend to be other than they are. As a result, your relationships will become sweeter, deeper, and fulfilling. You have the potential to embody the Divine Feminine in multiple facets, and when you do, you'll have no regrets for daring to take the plunge.

An Inclusive Guide to Identifying Who You Are: Maiden, Mother, Wild Woman, or Crone

Once more, you aren't excluded from channeling the Divine Feminine energy in your life by virtue of your gender. Regardless of how you identify, the odds are you are expressing one or a combination of the four main archetypes. But how do you determine which one you are? Use this guide to help you.

Begin by considering the things you value most in life. Your values will hint at the archetype you embody. If innocence matters to you more than anything else, then clearly, you are the Maiden. If you often find yourself taking on the role of a nurturer, you are the Mother. If you're in a phase of life when nothing matters to you more than your freedom, and you are relentlessly going after your passions, then the odds are you are the Wild Woman. What if you find that you're being more discerning as you make your choices and you've come to a place of genuine acceptance? Then, you're in touch with your inner Crone.

Look closely at where you currently are in life. In particular, what goals have you set for yourself? You embody the Maiden if you've decided to take on new adventures without reservations. You have her zest for life, untamed by disappointment. Is your desire to be a caring person? Are you building something, whether a family, relationships, or projects? Then, you are in your Mother energy. If you constantly throw yourself into the unexplored with reckless abandon, then you're being the Wild Woman. If you have to pause and reflect before taking action, seeking deeper meaning in your choices and your place in life, then you are in your Crone energy.

Examine your relationships with others in your life. As the Maiden, you're more likely to be curious and playful about connecting with new people and engaging with those you already know. As the Mother, you're the one people turn to whenever they need comfort, stability, and support. When you are the Wild Woman, while you enjoy your interactions with others, you are careful to ensure they do not dampen your passion, nor do you let them hinder your independence and freedom. As the Crone, you are the person in the friend group that everyone else turns to whenever they need advice to help them navigate difficult situations. You're the mentor. People in your life recognize your experience and wisdom, and they trust your guidance will be safe and sound.

Notice the activities and interests that give you pleasure and energy. Since the Maiden represents the start of life's cycle, she loves to learn new skills. If that's where you're at, then that's the energy you're embodying, and the only thing you're interested in is the growth that comes from learning. Do you find yourself drawn to activities where you play the role of the nurturer? Do you love helping people piece themselves together? Are you interested in bringing projects to completion? You're being the Mother.

As a Wild Woman, you refuse to be a part of anything that doesn't make your heart sing. Everything you're doing now brings you joy or is geared toward fulfilling your heart's desires. If you are more interested in activities that help you discover wisdom and apply the knowledge you've gathered practically, you're being the Crone. You're not in a hurry to get involved in things you don't care about.

Ask yourself what you're most afraid of and what your highest aspirations are. Are you terrified of never getting started on things that matter to you? Do you worry you'll never discover all life has to offer? You may be in your Maiden phase. If what scares you the most is the idea of having to let go or not controlling your life, then you may be exuding Mother energy. As a Wild Woman, nothing alarms you more than the thought of commitment because it means you'll lose your freedom and be tethered to one spot, which is the complete antithesis of this archetype's energy.

Next, consider your aspirations. The Maiden longs for growth. She knows there's so much more she could be. She realizes the only way to grow is to have experiences that are new to her. The Mother has done her exploring and now seeks more stability in her life, so if this is you, you're more interested in creating a rock-solid base for yourself. As the Wild Woman, you find that you are ready to be your truest, authentic self, which means becoming selfish — in a good way. You recognize it is time to give back to yourself. If you're the Crone, you desire to find inner peace and live a life that inspires all.

Practices for Integrating Your Dominant Feminine Archetype

For the Maiden:

1. Dedicate yourself to the practice of daily journaling. Why? As you journal, you discover more of who you are, which gives you a clue about what you should explore in your life. All you need is 15 minutes every day to enjoy the magical benefits of journaling. So, write about every new idea you have in your journal, what might have piqued your interest lately, how you plan to pursue said interest, and what you hope to accomplish for the day. Also, take five to 10 minutes at night to write in your journal, reflecting on how your day went and if it aligned with the goals you set for yourself at the start. Alternatively, you may prefer to use your night-time journaling to set your goals for the next day.
2. Make a list of everything that interests you and select what you'd like to make a hobby. You'll find the best things to pursue are completely brand new to you, as this will fuel your sense of wonder and your desire to explore the chosen subject further and your self-expression through that medium.
3. Think of one thing you could do to be kind to someone else every day. Ideally, they shouldn't be able to pay you back, and you shouldn't use your kindness as a bargaining chip either. You don't have to break the bank to be kind. A thoughtful compliment, a handwritten note of appreciation, or the

willingness to volunteer your time and attention toward a cause or someone is an excellent place to start.

Mantra: *"I satisfy my curiosity and embrace all possibilities."*

For the Mother:
1. Always keep your space clutter-free and organized, as this helps you feel in touch with your Mother energy. You'll benefit a lot by placing touches of nature around your home. Do you live with others? You'll benefit from having a special space decorated to your tastes, allowing you to return to embodying the Mother's vibe whenever you feel out of it.
2. You may find fulfillment in feeding others good, nutritious meals. Even if there's no one living with you, you can be Mother to yourself by taking care of nutritional needs, lovingly making them from scratch. When others are present, create a loving space of generosity and sharing by having everyone dine together in a grateful, mindful space.
3. Come up with ways you can be supportive of others around you, and see how you can show up for them as a mother would. You can do this in simple ways, like listening to someone with no judgment or observing the people in your life and offering them words or acts of service you know would make their lives easier to bear. Never miss the chance to demonstrate empathy. When you can't find an opportunity, you can always make one by being proactive and acting compassionately rather than waiting to be asked for help.

Mantra: *"I nurture myself and others. I am safety, peace, warmth, and love."*

For the Wild Woman:
1. Consider activities that will center you in your body. The more you have to move, the better. So, try yoga, take up dancing, go for long hikes through nature, or if you're daring, try rock climbing, paragliding, etc.
2. Make a commitment to yourself never to speak anything that isn't the truth, and never apologize for saying things truthfully, as they are. Rather than suppress yourself, allow your creativity to run wild and free, and should it bump up against obstacles in the arbitrary norms society uses to dampen your spirit, go full

throttle by leaning into being more of who you are without reservations.

3. Decide to be spontaneous. If you're invited somewhere, say yes, regardless of your plans (as long as it rings your bells, of course). Wholeheartedly embrace opportunities to abandon your comfort zone. Never pause to think it through. Instead, trust that the magic of the Wild Woman will lead you to pleasant places and wonderful surprises.

Mantra: *"I feed my passion. I honor my freedom. I follow my heart with joy and abandon."*

For the Crone:

1. Prioritize silence. Make time each day to think about what you've learned or are learning, how you're faring, and where you're headed. Walking through nature or just sitting with it around you is excellent for these self-reflection sessions. You'll gain a lot from meditation. So, sit in silence for at least 10 to 15 minutes daily, allowing thoughts to come and go without latching on to or engaging them.

2. You should connect with mentors and the elders around you if you haven't already. They have much wisdom to share, and the more you talk with them, the more their knowledge will rub off on you. You'll discover you don't have to make mistakes when you can learn from the experiences of others who have already taken the paths you're considering. Don't just take and take without giving back when you're with them. Share what you've learned, too. Your interactions with these precious souls should be balanced, nurturing everyone.

3. Spend time contemplating that everything in life is powered by the mechanics of cycles. Nothing stays the same forever. In other words, you can ponder life and death, beginnings and endings, the times you should hold on versus the times you should release and let go of things. It helps you find inner peace and keeps you from spiraling into a negative thought vortex about the "evil" of endings. After all, every end is a new beginning worthy of acceptance and celebration.

Mantra: *"I accept life. I express wisdom. I'm at peace with endings and beginnings."*

How to Embrace and Transmute Your Shadow Traits

Regardless of the Divine Feminine archetype you're embodying, more often than not, you'll have shadow traits that overtake your light aspects. How do you handle it when this happens? Here are some general tips:

1. Accept that these shadow traits are part and parcel of who you are. If you can't, they'll appear to hold you hostage. There's no way you'll learn what triggers you to express these dark aspects, let alone check them.
2. Become more self-aware by using meditation, contemplation, and journaling, among other similar practices, to get in touch with your authentic self. These tools will help you learn who you are, what you feel, what you think, and why you act the way you do. This is necessary before you can embrace your shadow side and transmute it.
3. Reframe your dark side by recognizing that it allows you to become the best version of yourself. If you are curious about it, you'll learn how it serves you, and you'll become a better person for it.
4. Pay attention to how you speak to yourself. If you're cruel and cutting, you need to cut that out right now and choose to be compassionate instead. If you wouldn't say it to a friend, you don't have permission to say it to yourself.

Here's specific advice for each of the 4 dominant Feminine archetypes.

For the Maiden: When your shadow side takes over, you're prone to being excessively dependent on others, acting irresponsibly, and being a little too naive for your own good. When you find yourself expressing these shadow traits, return to being curious. Become passionate about figuring things out for yourself. Curiosity will help you deal with your naivety, as you'll learn what you need to progress in life. If you're overwhelmed, don't be afraid to ask for help, but don't play the damsel in distress, either. You should always do your part to improve your situation. When you inevitably make mistakes (everyone does), be quick to take responsibility for your choices and turn your attention to seeking solutions.

For the Mother: As your shadow self, you tend to be overprotective. Naturally, this means you'll do what you think you must to keep the people you love safe. So, what's the problem here? Your overprotectiveness causes you to become manipulative. Eventually, when the people around you have had enough, they'll feel smothered by you. Therefore, your task is to learn to draw the line not just for others but for yourself. You can help so much, but no further. You must realize that people are autonomous beings who can and will make their own decisions, regardless of your advice or opinions.

So, practice trusting others and be deliberate about letting go when you sense you're being strong-handed or manipulative. Rather than be overprotective, recognize the independence of others and honor it. Rather than mentally strongarm someone into doing what you want through manipulation, communicate your concerns using reason and then get your hands off the wheel. Rather than smother people, give them the room to breathe and figure things out for themselves because this is the only way they'll grow.

For the Wild Woman: Wildness is fun, but when it gets out of hand, you can become a tad too reckless — some would argue, to the point of being destructive. You even sabotage yourself in the process. How can you combat this dark side? Learn to become more strategic in deciding what's worth the risk and what isn't. Take that wild, beautiful energy of yours and deliberately channel it only to constructive ends. The hallmarks of this archetype are adventure and spontaneity, two things that guarantee mistakes will be made. So, when you realize you've missed the mark, own your mistake. Recognize that accepting responsibility for things not going as you prefer isn't an indictment of who you are or your intrinsic value.

The transmutation work set out for you is to tame your recklessness unless and until you have enough information to unleash it however you please. Take your tendency to destroy and shift it toward creating, whether a project, a new skill, or connections with others. As for your self-sabotaging aspect, it can easily be quelled when you choose to be compassionate and kind to yourself, forgiving yourself of everything you hold against you. After all, you made the best choices you could make at the time with the information and your state of mind. Things may not pan out, but it doesn't mean you should keep your perceived flaws hanging over your head like a guillotine.

For the Crone: Your shadow self prefers to disconnect from others, isolating herself completely so no one can reach her. You're full of cynicism in this state, never expecting anything good from anyone or any situation. You are too rigid, set in your ways, and unwilling to try something new (even if it could be better than whatever you have going on right now). You have to "find the funny" in life, no matter how dark it may seem. There's always something to laugh at, but you have to be looking for it first. You'll benefit tremendously from accepting that things change and even more so from actively working to create a community of people with a shared vision.

Your cynicism can and should be transmuted into wisdom. A crucial part of wisdom is discernment, which is instrumental in helping you understand who and what to trust. You have this ability within you, and the more you work with it, the more you'll count on yourself. Once you trust yourself, your cynicism will melt because you'll realize that even if others prove to be something other than they seemed initially, you will do the right thing for yourself by walking away and asserting your boundaries. Choose to be flexible. Think about the arbitrary dos and don'ts you've set for yourself and question them. Be willing to learn new ways of being and living. You'll love it.

The World within and the World without

Embodying and expressing your feminine energy highly depends on two environments: the one in your mind and the one around you. You're far more likely to truly express yourself when these two environments are harmonious, allowing you to honor the Divine Feminine. So, here are ways to set up sacred spaces where you can rejuvenate and practice self-reflection:

Creating a space to focus affects your ability to focus.
https://www.pexels.com/photo/woman-meditating-with-candles-and-incense-3822864/

- **Pick a Spot in Your Home You Can Claim as Your Own:** Choose somewhere everyone knows they must avoid, as it is your private place. This space should have your personal effects and decorations that remind you of your archetype. You may want to decorate it with unique stones, crystals, plants, sculptures, wind chimes, or anything else you feel matches your archetype's vibe. This place must be quiet, or at least it should have an ambient sound that won't distract you from your spiritual and self-reflection practices.

- **Set up an Altar in This Space:** You don't have to if you don't want to, but altars are lovely because they act as an energetic magnet, drawing your focus to your meditation, contemplation, journaling, and rituals while also pulling the Divine Feminine energy so it feels real to you. Your altar could have statues or pictures of the goddesses you are drawn to, precious stones, beautiful flowers, books that hold meaning for you and remind you of who you are, and anything else your heart tells you would fit on it. You could have candles, which should only ever be lit when you can keep an eye on them. Scented candles would be an awesome addition to your altar for a more sensory experience.

- **Prepare Your Mind and Heart:** For your mental and emotional "environment," you should always leave all your troubles behind when it's time to do your work, whether a ritual, shadow work, meditation, or anything else. If you bring said troubles with you, it should be intentional, with the understanding that you will transmute them into better outcomes through your rituals. In other words, you should intend that the Divine Feminine will help you with whatever's bothering you. This intention will help you shift from an energy of fear, anxiety, and worry to peace, gratitude, and trust that the loving Mother Goddess has already sorted it all out.

Before wrapping up this chapter, there's one point to always keep in mind: You will have a more profound connection with the Divine Feminine when you accept that you're worthy. You're worthy of having the gift of life. You're worthy of her love, attention, and other gifts for the simple fact that you exist. You don't need to do, be, or have some extra special, ephemeral quality to experience this energy's reality and love in your life.

Well, there is one thing you must do: Discover your self-worth. By using the practical exercises in this chapter, you'll surely find it. Here's something even cooler: *You'll discover your worth has no end or depth. Your self-worth is infinite.* Begin now by using the advice you've received so far. Begin loving your magnificent self; begin creating as though you could never create badly, and amaze yourself with just how much compassion you can extend to yourself — even when your ego tries to convince you that you're not so hot.

Chapter 4: Sacred Union Within: Balancing Your Energies

Since you now know that the Divine Feminine and the Divine Masculine exist in everyone, and you've begun tapping into the Divine Feminine, it will be easier for you to let the light of the Divine wisdom within you illuminate your path. What happens next? Well, you need to understand the core of each energy, how they play out, and what makes them distinct. Armed with this information, you'll be able to tell when you're out of balance, living a life that skews more toward one energy than the other. Therefore, it will be easier for you to find your center, and as a result, your spiritual growth and general well-being will astound you.

Balance your divine feminine and masculine energies.
https://easy-peasy.ai/ai-image-generator/images/understanding-sex-and-gender-visual-explanation

The Concept of Duality

Simply observing the world around you should tell you there's something off about the idea that there is only one God that has only masculine attributes. The same oddity should strike you even when you encounter religions or practices claiming this God is truly a goddess and there is none other besides her. Observe life, and you'll find that everything has its polar opposite — although "opposite" is not necessarily the best way to put it.

You see, a thing and its opposite are really one and the same. If you have a dime, just because it has heads and tails doesn't mean you have two dimes. You understand this truth applies to everything in life, even if you have been conscious of it. Seeming opposites are merely the same thing on the extremes of a spectrum.

The same can be said for divinity.

For far too long, many have assumed that God is masculine, but you now understand that God is both masculine and feminine. The creative force responsible for all of life carries the duality mirrored in its creation.

The universe is ruled by cycles and seasons. This progression from cycle to cycle happens even when expressing divinity as masculine or feminine. The Divine Masculine has taken precedence over the Divine Feminine, ruling supreme for at least 25,920 years on Earth. This alternating cycle is real, so much so it has its own name: the Precession of the Equinoxes. Without fail, the Earth journeys through every Zodiac sign, taking at least 2,152 years to move from one sign to the next. By the time this little blue dot completes its journey through every astrological house, at least 25,000 years have passed.

As it turns out, you are fortunate enough to live during a time when the masculine energy is finishing its course and witness humanity's rise to a new level of awareness. In this era, the Age of Aquarius, all souls awaken to a higher and deeper understanding of life they have always carried within but have been unaware of for too long. It is said that this is when the 5th dimension becomes real to everyone. It's when the Divine Feminine and the Divine Masculine express themselves in harmony with one another and every heart and soul. You're already experiencing this transformation, and this book you are reading is evidence.

What Is the Divine Masculine?

The Divine Masculine is a core part of the universe, just as the Divine Feminine is. In the same way that it is impossible to conceive a child without the male and female reproductive cells, it is impossible to conceive a universe without the Divine Masculine and the Divine Feminine working in harmony. You seek to understand what the Divine Masculine is all about. There's no better way to do so than by analyzing its traits.

- **Assertiveness:** The Divine Masculine balances the passivity of the Divine Feminine. Assertion is the quality of doing what needs to be done to get the required results. In the never-ending debate between sexes, assertiveness has often been misconstrued as dominance, but it's not the same thing. Dominance seeks to control through force by any means necessary, with no regard for others, which is toxic masculinity at its finest. It's one way the shadow side of masculine archetypes shows up. It's nothing to do with the Divine Masculine. However, the assertion is about persistence and consistency.

- **Determination:** The Divine Masculine is goal-oriented and relentless in its desire to accomplish set goals. Contrast this with the Divine Feminine, which is laid back, working with emotions and introspection to allow things to come rather than to chase after them. It would be impossible to accomplish your dreams without determination, one of the Divine Masculine's gifts.

- **Action:** The Divine Masculine takes action. It does not remain passive. Passivity is a trait of the Divine Feminine. You can see this mirrored in how men and women relate to one another. In the most traditional sense, the masculine goes after the feminine heart, never stopping until it is secured. Even in nontraditional relationship dynamics, the same holds true. The Divine Masculine energy is about action through movement.

- **Goal-Focused:** The point of the Divine Masculine's action is to accomplish goals. When you are in your masculine energy, you make things happen. You focus on your goals and don't stop until you see them through.

- **Risk-Taking:** Masculine energy is about taking risks, while feminine energy is about remaining safe and pragmatic. There's no way to accomplish your goals if you're not willing to put something on the line, knowing there's a chance this sacrifice may not pay off. Yet, this willingness to take risks is a necessary trait if you are to succeed in life.
- **Protection and Provision:** Where the Divine Feminine nurtures, the Divine Masculine protects. This isn't to imply some foolishness like the term "the weaker sex" holds water. It's the natural role of the Divine Masculine to offer protection. The Divine Masculine naturally sees to it that everyone is provided for through action.
- **Leadership:** The Divine Masculine energy powers leadership. When you have to decide, you're leading, which can only be effectively accomplished when you're in touch with your inner masculine self.
- **Strength and Courage:** Masculinity is about strength in all forms and the willingness to combine that strength with courageous action to accomplish whatever needs to be done despite possible danger or risk.

Signs of Imbalance

When individuals or the human collective lean more toward one divine energy over another, there are unmistakable signs. Look around you. You can clearly see the dark manifestations of the shadow or unhealed aspect of the Divine Masculine. People are stressed, burned out, and unable to find joy in life anymore because they've lost sight of what's important. Perhaps you, too, may have felt this way. How are you in your relationships with others? Do you have trouble setting boundaries, and others walk all over you, or you may disrespect others' boundaries, causing what could otherwise have been a great relationship to become unhealthy and toxic?

People are afraid of being vulnerable these days. They think it's a sign of weakness, so to keep themselves "safe," they repress everything they feel. The result? Everyone walks around in their own little bubbles, isolated from everyone else. The lack of connection is a symptom of a world sorely lacking in empathy, kindness, and compassion. What about the little moments of positivity or the pockets of people who appear to push for a brighter world? Look closer, and you'll find that, in truth, there's nothing "positive" about the positivity brand they push. It's toxic, nothing more than tinsel, a veneer meant to make people shut their pain within even though it eats away at them.

Not having the proper balance between the Divine Masculine and the Divine Feminine energy in your life means you cannot distinguish between your energy and another person's. In other words, you don't have energetic or emotional boundaries, so you take on other people's feelings as if they were yours, which is draining. Even if you are more empathetic than most, you will benefit from learning how to protect your energy and to tell when you're feeling someone else's emotions rather than yours.

The best way to handle this is by deliberately balancing both aspects within yourself. If you don't, you'll find that you abandon yourself emotionally. When you have to express your needs, you don't do so healthily. You want to speak the truth but can't because you're terrified about putting yourself first, even though it's sometimes necessary. Does all this sound familiar?

Another sign is the constant push for productivity, to the detriment of other aspects of your life. Every other influencer or *"furu"* (another way to say "fake guru") yells at you from the YouTube mountains to the TikTok valleys that you must hustle. "You're sleeping too much," is what they say about getting regular hours of sleep. "You're not pushing hard enough," they preach at you, never mind that you've put your blood, sweat, and tears into making these "dreams" you've been sold as the ideal to happen while seeing little to no results – usually due to constantly moving the goalposts. The push for productivity is so bad that people don't take care of themselves anymore. They don't care for their mental or physical health, as they worship at the altar of the almighty dollar in the cathedral of capitalism. Perhaps you, too, are noticing the futility of it all, which is why you've answered the Divine Feminine call.

Things don't look great for the collective either, not when it comes to the imbalance of energies. War is the order of the day. Once upon a time, world leaders would at least put up a facade of caring, as though war were an ugly business they didn't want to be part of but found themselves in the middle of out of necessity. Now? They don't even bother with putting on their makeup and costumes properly. The media's lies are more glaringly obvious than ever, causing an overall feeling of "Us against them."

Even the "us's" have divisions among themselves. This ethos results from having lived far too long, completely ignoring one energy and favoring the other. You may think the solution is a pendulum swing to the other side, to the other extreme where the matriarchy is in charge, and the Divine Feminine is only acknowledged, but that isn't it either. That could easily lead to stagnation, an inability to seek the new and embrace change, and other issues just as bad as being in a world high on spiritual testosterone.

Misconceptions on Balancing the Feminine and Masculine

Here's a quick look at some of the misconceptions people have about what it means to balance the feminine and the masculine:

1. "Balance would lead to everyone being the same, which would make the world a boring place and eventually stagnate progress." This isn't true. There's room for individuality even as people learn to balance both sides. You won't lose yourself, so don't worry.
2. "Once you find balance, you remain in that state for the rest of your life." The truth is you'll always fluctuate in the degree to which you express one energy over another. It's a lifelong practice.
3. "You have to be in a conventional relationship to find this balance." While you can learn a lot about balancing yourself in a relationship, you don't need a partner before you learn to find balance. You're already in a relationship with yourself. Finding a balance between both energies is something you'll do by becoming more self-aware and paying attention to how you relate to yourself.

These are a few misconceptions about balancing the Divine Feminine and Divine Masculine energies. Still, they're some of the more problematic ones that could impede your progress if you believe them. You'll have better physical and mental health by keeping these energies balanced. The power of the divine will become a real, undeniable force in your life you'll learn to rely on for everything you need.

Exercises for Balancing Your Masculine and Feminine Energies

The following techniques and exercises will help you find the balance between your expression of the Divine Feminine and Divine Masculine in your daily life.

Use Breathwork: Breathwork refers to special breathing techniques that alter your state of consciousness and allow you to grasp spiritual ideas better than you would in a regular waking state. It can change your physiology as well as your mind for the better. One useful technique is alternate nostril breathing.

Alternative nostril breathing.
https://www.pexels.com/photo/a-woman-doing-nostril-breathing-6648567/

Here's how it works:

1. If you're not already wearing something comfy, do that now.
2. Find a quiet place where you won't be distracted or disturbed. Shut your eyes as you sit in a comfortable position. You'll need about five to 10 minutes of uninterrupted time.
3. Shut your eyes, use your right thumb, and press against your right nostril, shutting off the airflow.
4. With your right nostril shut, take a deep breath through the left one.

5. Release your right nostril so it's open again.
6. Using your ring finger, press down on your left nostril to shut it.
7. Exhale through your right nostril.
8. Repeat this sequence for the next five to 10 minutes.

The beautiful thing about alternate nostril breathing is it helps you balance both hemispheres of your brain, which correlate to the masculine and feminine energies.

Practice Self-Reflective Journaling: This is journaling with a twist. Rather than document what happened each day, write about your feelings concerning the predominant energy you embody. So, even if you write about daily occurrences, do it in the context of how much you express the Divine Feminine and Divine Masculine in balance. As you journal, think about the parts of your life where you sense there might be an imbalance. Pay attention to aspects of your life where you push yourself harder than necessary and find it tough to draw the line with others or express what you need from them. You'll find it helpful to write about your emotions and document how often you were in touch with your intuition and followed it.

Self-reflective journaling should be a daily exercise for effective results.
https://www.pexels.com/photo/elderly-woman-writing-her-diary-while-smiling-7260644/

Get Creative: Creatively expressing yourself is another excellent way to restore the balance between these energies. Consider activities that force you to maintain your focus and discipline your mind or body to channel more of the Divine Masculine. You could learn a new technical skill, play chess, work out, etc. If you sense you could use more of the Divine Feminine, you should try singing, dancing, writing, painting, sculpting, and other creative endeavors.

Develop Body Awareness: Take up yoga. It is an excellent activity that forces you out of your head and into your body. Certain poses are meant to awaken the Divine Masculine within you, while others will stir the Divine Feminine. An excellent yoga instructor will know how to blend both into a routine.

Reframe Old Wounds: Sometimes, the imbalances of these divine energies are caused by experiences you may have had in the past that traumatized or gave you a mindset that's been a handicap to you. In this instance, it would be most beneficial to dig deep into your past to discover why you've become dependent on one form of energy or the other.

Once you have identified these landmark experiences, you have a new task: You must reframe them to make them positive. You take the negative energy and transmute it using understanding and compassion toward yourself. This doesn't mean you should deny that these things happened or gaslight yourself into thinking that it wasn't that bad. However, you become a researcher keenly on the lookout for the silver linings, the good within the bad. So, how do you find the gold in your pain? By asking yourself what lessons you've learned and how they empower you today.

Let Nature Be Your Ally: The more time you spend in nature, the more balanced you will become because nature does not know how to exist without balance. Whether in your modern spartan apartment several hundreds of floors above the hubbub of humanity and the din of daily life or deep in the heart of the Amazon, you will always be a part of nature. However, deliberately putting yourself in touch with nature accelerates balancing your energies. You can hike, sit on the beach and watch the ocean, walk barefoot on natural ground, lie on your back on the grass, use your imagination, or do whatever else you desire to connect with nature.

Practice Meditation Daily: Meditation may not be easy at first, but it is simple. All you need is five to 10 minutes in a quiet place. Wear comfortable clothing, sit or lie down, and shut your eyes. Keep your attention on your breathing for as long as you can. If you've never done this before, the odds are you will constantly get distracted. This does not mean you're doing anything wrong. It's actually awesome that you are becoming aware of how often your mind jumps from topic to topic. Whenever you notice that you have stopped focusing on your breathing, simply acknowledge whatever thought you have in your mind and gently release it as you return to your breath. You shouldn't be harsh on yourself, even if you get distracted every other second. With consistent practice, you'll become better at maintaining awareness of your thoughts.

Work with Acupuncture and Reiki: Acupuncture can help you get rid of imbalances in the energetic flow in your body's meridians. Reiki is another way to accomplish this by moving stuck energy so there's free flow all through your chakra system and imbalances are sorted out. You'll need to work with a qualified practitioner if you choose to explore these healing modalities to sort out the imbalance between your inner masculine and feminine aspects.

Chapter 5: You're Never Alone — Spirit Guides

Whether or not you've been aware of it, you've never been alone. You've always had divine assistance waiting for you to acknowledge and accept. This help is offered to you by your spirit guides. But who exactly are these beings, and how do they make your life better?

You've always had divine assistance waiting for you to acknowledge and accept.
https://pixabay.com/photos/book-cover-holy-spiritual-light-4393603/

What Are Spirit Guides?

Your spirit guides are precisely what they sound like. They are guides that exist in spirit form, so they are not visible to the naked eye unless you have the gift of an awakened third-eye chakra. In pretty much the same way that air exists but cannot be seen, your spirit guides are real, even if you can't see or sense them just yet. As you feel the effect of air, you can pick up on the presence and workings of your guides in your life if you're sensitive to them or become observant. No one knows better than your spirit guides what would serve your highest purpose. No one could possibly offer you better advice than them.

If you are confused because you have multiple options, your spirit guides can give you clarity to help you choose the best path for your intentions. Not only are they excellent advisors, but they also help you to plan, organize, and strategize your life. If you'd like to accomplish something by reaching out to them, they can help you implement your goals. Your spirit guides also play the all-important role of working with the spirit guides of others around you so that the best outcome for everyone is always accomplished — provided you ask for their help. They won't interfere or do anything without your permission because otherwise, their actions would be in violation of your sacred free will.

These amazing beings have been with you ever since you were born, whether or not you were aware of them. Not only do they know your present life like the back of their hands, but they also know your past lives. They understand how all these lives intertwine and affect one another. There's no better source to help you understand the challenges you face and the opportunities you may be missing out on than your spirit guides and their deep well of knowledge. Think of them as energetic encyclopedias on everything concerning your past, present, and future.

Different Kinds of Spirit Guides and Their Roles

Guardian Angels: These guides are known as "life guides" because they accompany you from before birth to after death, from one incarnation to the next. Anytime you feel confused about something, they're there to offer you the best advice. They're the reason you get the sense that you shouldn't be walking down a particular street at a specific time, even if you've always done so with no problems. They give you intuitive nudges to keep you out of trouble and lead you where you want to go.

These beings are like best friends who never judge you and are always there for you. You could argue they're even better than friends because they never take their eyes off you and don't have to sleep or take a day off from work. So, if you're ever in a sticky situation, know that you no longer have to be afraid. You can confirm the reality of these guides by telling them exactly how you want them to help you and watch in amazement as everything you ask for plays out beautifully, thanks to their intervention.

Archangels: The archangels have their work cut out for them across various heavenly realms. They are powerful angels who are not to be trifled with. Why? Because, unlike regular angels and guides, they are tasked with the job of caring for everything affecting every world, known and unknown, seen and unseen. Even in the darkest of times, they ensure humans do not annihilate themselves. They spread their loving kindness and warmth as an energetic shield protecting people from the darkness.

Some people assume because the archangels have a broader scope of affairs to handle, they should never be called on for help. However, this is not the case. You cannot think of these beings as limited in space and time like humans. They can be everywhere, all at once. You are part of the world they care for, so you can call out to them if you're intuitively led to.

Spirit Animals: The interesting thing about spirit animals is that they embody the energy of the animal form they take. Your spirit animal is a source of strength you can draw from whenever you face challenges and tough times. Typically, the spirit animal has a unique quality, resilience, which is necessary for your particular life path. It is not unheard of to have more than one spirit animal or to have your spirit animal change from time to time.

Spirit animals embody energy and strength and guide us.
https://www.wallpaperflare.com/owls-pharaoh-eagle-owl-eyes-bird-one-animal-animal-wildlife-wallpaper-warod

Of what use are these spirit guides, you wonder? Well, you merely need to think about the attributes of each animal to appreciate what they bring to the table. For instance, the bear has unparalleled strength and the wisdom to hibernate when it's time. The snake is representative of wisdom and regenerative power. The peacock teaches you to show your authentic self fully, with no apologies, and to be proud of who you are. The butterfly is the epitome of the power of transformation. Some people refer to these beings as animal totems. Bringing them to mind or asking for their help will yield good results.

Ancestral Spirits: Your ancestors can also act as spirit guides. They are invested in your affairs because you are their direct descendant. They've had to deal with the same struggles and challenges as you. Since they've already walked your path, they have wisdom and lessons to teach, benefiting you in particular. Your ancestors are an excellent support system. You can draw from their strength and wisdom whenever you need to. Call on them if you feel you could use more courage or bravery. They are fiercely protective of their own. If you choose to interact with your ancestors, it is best to specify that you only want to work with those who have your best interests at heart. Remember, your ancestors were once human, which means, like humans, some may be mischievous at best or downright awful at worst. Why does this matter? Imagine having a serial killer or cult leader as one of your ancestors. Not all ancestors have good intentions. Crossing over to the other side does not necessarily indicate that they have become good people, so you must be specific about who's allowed in your life and who isn't.

Ascended Masters: Once upon a time, ascended masters lived on Earth, just as you do. They've experienced many incarnations and learned so much. They've transcended the need to reincarnate on Earth. Therefore, they serve on a spiritual plane, helping all humanity to navigate life's many challenges. They offer wisdom beyond anything imaginable.

If you connect with ascended masters, they can help you understand your path and how to develop spiritually. These masters have been known to visit people in their dreams, teaching and offering insightful information about specific situations they're experiencing in their waking lives.

Healing Spirits and Messenger Spirits: The spirits' roles are exactly as their names suggest. Healing spirits are there to help you whenever you're mentally, physically, or emotionally down. They revive and rejuvenate your soul, soothing your body, mind, and heart.

As for the messenger spirits, they show up with important pieces of information to help you along your path. Sometimes, they'll use your dreams – and other times, they'll orchestrate engaging experiences that, upon closer inspection, will reveal a deep, meaningful message for you.

Elementals: These are the spirits that are within all of nature. They are in water, fire, air, and Earth. They're in every river, plant, ocean, mountain, etc. They remind you to get in touch with nature, to bring your soul into balance whenever you have lost your way.

Now you know about the many spirit guides available, you should realize that you have access to them all, as they play unique, essential roles in your life.

How Spirit Guides Communicate with You

Spirits always have something for those who have eyes to see and ears to hear. The trouble is that not many people understand when their spirit guides are communicating with them. It's far more common to dismiss their attempts at reaching out as nothing more than mere coincidence. You're not going to make that mistake because you need to hear whatever messages they have for you. Once you become adept at knowing when they're communicating with you and reaching out to them in turn, you can seek their guidance on finding the balance between the Divine Feminine and Divine Masculine in your life. So, here's how to discern that your spirit guides are communicating with you.

You Experience Synchronicity: Synchronicity is the union of a series of unlikely events in time and space in a way that's profoundly meaningful to the person witnessing them. Others may consider these as mere coincidences, but these synchronicities have meaning for you. People in touch with the Divine Spirit understand that there's no such thing as a coincidence. The minute you accept this by default, you'll notice more synchronicity in your life as your guides attempt to reach out to you.

What do these synchronicities look like? You may notice you keep waking up at specific times or looking at the clock just when it has a precise set of numbers, like 11:11 or 4:44. You may see these numbers showing up often on receipts, on license plates, as a perfectly positioned group of football players with their jersey numbers creating that number, etc. You could even hear these numbers in random conversations that have nothing to do with you or turn on the TV just in time to see someone holding up a placard with that number.

Synchronicity could also be a repetition of a certain event in various ways. For instance, Allison reported that she had experienced flooding in her house because of a broken pipe, only for her to get to work the next day and find that the office bathroom had suffered a similar fate. Her guides definitely wanted her to pay attention to something. Curious, she asked for guidance and received her answer in a dream. She was told she would experience a financial emergency but that it was imperative to keep positive through it all because if she did, something wonderful would happen after upgrading her financial status.

The next day, her relative needed to be bailed out, which cost more money than Allison could afford to spare without becoming uncomfortable. Still, she did what she could to help. No less than a week later, this same relative had a windfall after winning the lottery. Feeling gratitude to Allison for bailing her out, she gave her ten times what she'd to bail her out.

Synchronicity also involves receiving answers to questions. You may ask about something bothering you, only to turn on the radio and hear a musician belting out the exact line of the song; that is the perfect, comforting answer. Here's another fun story: Blake feels down about his life and alone. He didn't have anyone he could reach out to due to a terrible falling out he'd had with family and friends resulting from a narcissist's smear campaign. He had a good cry in a café's bathroom and asked for a sign that things would work out fine. When he was done, he splashed water on his face to wash away his tears.

As he opened the door to head back out, another man rushed in, and the two collided, their heads bumping against each other. The man, embarrassed, apologized profusely to Blake, who stood there, staring at the newcomer in awestruck silence. Why? Well, this man wore a T-shirt with these words written in bold lettering: "You'll Never Walk Alone!" To anyone else, that meant nothing. But for Blake, the moment was poignant. As if confirming, a day later, the narcissist who ruined his life was caught in a scandal that unraveled and revealed their many lies, vindicating Blake and restoring his connection with his loved ones.

You Encounter Certain Animals: You usually spot them in the weirdest places, and it feels like they've been waiting there just for you and no one else to find them. They may stare a little longer than an animal ordinarily would at a human.

Encountering animals in weird places can mean that your spirit guides are trying to communicate with you.

https://unsplash.com/photos/brown-fox-on-snow-field-xUUZcpQlqpM?utm_content=creditShareLink&utm_medium=referral&utm_source=unsplash

You Dream of Your Guides: Guides can show up in your dreams to teach, comfort, warn, clarify, etc. These dreams don't feel ordinary. You wake up with the undeniable knowledge that you met your guide.

They'll Call Your Name or Touch You: Some people have a negative mindset about this, so their belief opens them up to trickster spirits. However, it's not weird to be woken up by your guide softly whispering your name in your ear (or loudly if they have to warn you of something). Sharon's friend Myron had told her that he never needed an alarm clock to wake up since he simply told his guides when he wanted to be up, and he'd be woken at that time or a few minutes before. Sharon thought her friend was nuts, but she was open-minded enough to try. She asked to be woken by 4:30 AM the next day. Sharon was awoken by a warm hand that, in her words, "felt full of love" as it gave her right shoulder a gentle squeeze. She looked at her phone, and sure enough, she watched the digital clock flip from 4:29 to 4:30. Since then, Sharon has actively pursued and developed her connection with her guides.

Your Ears Ring: Contrary to what the skeptics think, this isn't tinnitus. You'll know it because when it happens, there's often something major going on around you, or you may have a thought that was so important your guides had to make you pause to pay attention. Whenever you hear that high-pitched sound, observe what's happening around you and ask yourself what you were thinking of when you heard it. After hearing that sound, follow whatever urge you have because it's your guide leading you away from danger or toward something extraordinary.

How to Develop Your Intuition and Receptivity to Understand Your Guides

You can follow these ten steps to help you tune in to your intuition, which is how your spirit guides reach out to you.

Meditate: Practice meditation every day to train your mind to get to and stay in the state that makes it easy to understand what your guides tell you.

Document Your Dreams: Keep your journal beside your bed. When you wake up, don't move, and don't plan your day in your mind. Instead, think about the last scene or feeling you remember from your dream, then work your way backward. When you can't remember anything more, open your eyes, grab your journal, and write your dreams down. Start with a keyword representing each scene in the dream before filling in the details. This way, you don't forget the rest of your dreams while writing one out. The more you do this, the better your dream recall will be, and the easier it will be for your guides to reach you through your dreams.

Make a List of Things You Want Your Guides to Take Care of: It could have two items or more. When you're done, address them as you would a friend, and ask them to help you handle what you want. Be sincere, respectful, and appreciative of them. The more you do, the stronger the link between you and your guides.

Be Expectant: If you've never done this before, expect that your guides will reach out to you. Don't question it, even if you don't get a response when you think you should. You may not receive an answer or a solution right away, but when you do, you'll find it's right on time and not a moment too soon or too late.

Thank Them Constantly: Think of the things in your life that have improved or are going well. The odds are high that your guides had something to do with it. So, make a point of thanking them each day, not only for what they've done and continue to do, but also for their selfless companionship. Your appreciation is magnetic, drawing your guides closer to you. It fires them up to the point where your conversations and interactions become a moment-to-moment thing.

Before moving on to the next chapter, you should know this: Yes, many naysayers say spirit guides are nothing more than a figment of imagination that desperately needs to be checked. However, there's only one way to refute these skeptical attacks. By putting everything you've learned here to work. Be prepared to be wowed by the reality of your guides. Think about what you hope to gain from this wonderful partnership you're about to become a conscious part of, and you're bound to succeed. Prioritize asking for their help balancing the Divine Feminine and Divine Masculine in your life. You won't be disappointed.

Chapter 6: Connecting with Your Allies

You now have the most relevant information about your spirit guides. So, it's time to get your hands in the clay and discover how you can establish a connection with these wonderful beings. In this chapter, you'll learn to sustain that connection even when life's vicissitudes attempt to pull you away from your spiritual relationships with these guides.

Connect with your spirit guides.
https://www.pexels.com/photo/woman-meditating-in-the-outdoors-2908175/

Preparing Your Mind and Spirit

If you've spent most of your life blissfully unaware of spiritual reality, you need to work on getting into the correct state of mind and spirit before connecting with your guides. Why does this matter? Skipping this important process would be like trying to see through glasses with lenses smeared with oil and dirt or eavesdrop on a conversation three rooms away while loud heavy metal music is blasted from massive speakers.

The oil, dirt, and metal music refer to the many beliefs and biases society has installed in your mind about the nature of reality, the existence of worlds beyond the physically observable one, and the feasibility of establishing contact with beings that, according to science, logic, and reason, don't exist.

One of the biggest mistakes you could make in grasping a spiritual concept like the Divine Feminine is to curve-fit spirit to matter. In other words, you cannot use physical rules and expectations as a basis to determine that spirituality is nonexistent hogwash. Many realize there's something off about the stories they've been fed since birth. Perhaps you were one of these people. Perhaps in the past, you noticed every time you had a question that would shatter your illusions about how reality works, you would get a spiritual or mental pop-up blocker, for lack of a better way to describe it.

This pop-up blocker is a carefully crafted line of logic or reason that immediately causes you to shut down your spiritual exploration. One of the most effective blockers is the "fact" that if it cannot be observed by the five senses or picked up by a scientific instrument, it must not exist. This is an arrogant approach to understanding things beyond the physical. It would be like using a thermometer to check the volume of sound or a noise meter to detect the temperature of water. In other words, how can you use physical instruments to measure or determine the existence of spiritual realities? Some things lie beyond the rigid straight lines of reason and logic —necessary for operating in this physical world but not in realms beyond. Until you are willing to accept this, you will not make much progress.

Two of the quickest ways to break through the persistent illusion of lies you've been sold is to practice meditation, which will increase your self-awareness, and to question everything, including your own thoughts — especially those you are 100% certain are true. Do not listen to derogatory, dismissive statements like "It's all in your head." The truth is, it really all is in your head, including your experience of the physical world. There is no way to perceive reality, physical or spiritual, other than through your awareness or consciousness. Quantum physicists are closer to this truth than other scientists. But that's not a matter to be concerned about; they will catch up eventually.

Now that you have the premise needed to experience your spirit guide's reality, you have to put in the work. The first step is to assume that what you have learned here is true and that you can experience it. You do not need to use logic or reason to justify this assumption because the odds are with your programming (especially if you grew up in the Western world rather than Africa or the East, where spirituality isn't scoffed at and is consciously experienced every day), you may be too doubtful to initiate the first contact with your guides.

So, pause for a moment and assume that the version of you who questioned spiritual affairs never existed, assuming that you've always understood the reality of things beyond what is observable with the physical senses. Done? Good. Here are other things to prepare your mind and spirit to commune with your guides.

Keep Your Mind Focused on Your Goal: More than anything else, you should hunger for a connection with the Divine. To sustain that hunger and passion for connecting with what is beyond you, you should do everything within your power to remind yourself of how important this goal is to you. If it means setting alarms throughout the day to remind you to check in with yourself, meditating, contemplating the existence of spiritual guides, or checking in with them, do it. An excellent way to ensure you remain focused is to set things up so that connecting with your spirit guides is the first thing on your mind in the morning and the last thing when you go to bed at night.

Set Your Intentions and Make Them as Clear as You Can: Some people ask for signs that their spirit guides exist, and that's all they ever get - signs and nothing more. However, if you want constant, ongoing dialogue between yourself and your spirit guides, you should be clear about that. The clearer you are about your intentions for establishing contact with your guides, the better your results will be.

You cannot ask for signs and then be upset when all you ever get is a barrage of 444s and 1111s. You must be clear about what you want. If you haven't figured it out yet, there's no rush. Take your time to create your intention to the letter, and then you may begin the process knowing that you'll achieve your spiritual goal in a matter of time.

Stay Open and Receptive: With your focus on your goal and your intentions crystal clear, you'll notice moments when you have an extra sense of presence and awareness. Some people have mistaken this for depersonalization or derealization, but that's not what it is. It's your spirit guides bringing the fullness of your awareness to the here and now. You cannot connect with them in your past or your future. You can only establish that connection in the now.

When you become more aware and present, you'll find it easier to let them help you. You'll hear them, and that's good because they're always ready to speak with you. However, if you shake off the feeling of "extra presence," you close yourself off from your guides. So, rather find a quiet place every time you feel this way and sit in silent meditation and expectation for at least fifteen minutes. Don't sit aimlessly. Instead, set an intention to receive and understand your guide's message clearly.

Guided Visualization to Initiate Contact with Your Guides

One of the best things to connect with your spiritual guides is to meditate daily. You can use the alternate breathing technique regularly to help you. Whatever you choose, always set your intention for the technique before you begin. Now, on to another powerful, potent tool to help you make your spirit guides as real as the words on this page.

Guided visualization is like meditation but with instructions. You can write and record your guided visualizations, but if you prefer, you could use one available for free online. The idea is that you will not merely be meditating but focusing on the instructions about what to do with your body and what to imagine as you meditate. Here is a simple one you can use right now. Since you cannot meditate while reading, record this first. Don't rush your recording so you have time to follow each instruction. When you're ready to use the guided visualization, ensure you're dressed comfortably and in a quiet space where you won't be disturbed. Switch off all devices. If you don't live alone, ask your people not to bother you until you let them know you're ready.

Instructions:
1. Sit on a chair or the mat.
2. Feel your body. Make adjustments until you feel comfortable, then close your eyes.
3. Now you're settled, part your lips slightly. You're going to breathe deeply in through your nose and out through your mouth. Your exhales may be longer than your inhales, and that's okay. For now, just enjoy breathing, allowing your body to flood with love and light as you inhale and allow it to relax as you exhale.
4. Notice how, with each breath, you sink deeper and deeper into your body, feeling relaxed and at ease, very present in the moment.
5. Now that your body is settled and your mind is quiet, imagine a beautiful place. It has to be somewhere that calls to you. It could be a mountain top, a beach, a garden, or a forest. It could be your childhood home or a particular time and place when you felt safest.
6. Imagine yourself walking down the path that leads to this peaceful place. Pay attention to the crunch beneath your feet as each hits the floor.
7. As you walk, you notice up ahead of you there's a figure. Something about them draws you. With each step, you feel the love coming from them toward you. This being is your spirit guide. There's no specific form your guide needs to take on. They'll choose something familiar and comfortable, so you needn't fear or worry.
8. As you draw closer, notice what they're wearing and how they look. Are they smiling? How do their eyes make you feel as they look upon you?
9. Now, you're slow to a stop as you stand before your guide. Their arms are spread out, beckoning you to hug them. You accept their invitation and embrace them, feeling the warmth, love, and light flowing from them into your body, mind, and spirit.
10. Now, you pull back and thank them for their presence. If you have any questions, you ask them and wait with them as they speak to you. They may simply project thoughts into your mind

if they don't use words. If what you receive in response feels more like energy or an emotion, you can trust that the matter you've brought forward is already resolved. You'll see or receive a clear answer in the days to come.
11. Offer your guide sincere thanks for their presence, support, and comfort. Embrace them once more. When you're ready, return your awareness to your body and how it feels. Notice your breath once more.
12. In five seconds, you will open your eyes feeling refreshed and rejuvenated, with your heart and mind at peace.
13. You're becoming more and more aware of your breath.
14. Your awareness of your body is increasing.
15. Now you're noticing the space you're in, becoming aware of sounds and sensations.
16. You're stirring, waking up.
17. You're fully present, joyful, and energized. Gently open your eyes.

What If You Can't Imagine? Some people don't have the ability to see things in their mind's eye. If this is you, no worries. You can still use guided visualization, but instead of trying to imagine a physical place, transport yourself mentally to a time in the past when you felt safe and hold on to the feeling. In other words, forget about visuals and focus on sensations, emotions, and sound.

Signs and Confirmations

As mentioned, your spirit guides are always ready to speak to you. Trust is essential if you intend to fully comprehend whatever they're sharing with you. You have to trust that your guides exist. Trust in the process of initiating contact, whether through meditation, guided visualization, or breathwork. Finally, trust they will make themselves known to you, should you intend it. Here are the signs you're developing a strong connection with your guides:

333

Repeated number sequences are one form of synchronicity you may see.
Pinterpandai.com, CC BY-SA 3.0 <https://creativecommons.org/licenses/by-sa/3.0>, via Wikimedia Commons: https://commons.wikimedia.org/wiki/File:333_Angel_Number.jpg

1. You see more synchronicities in your life, especially with the repeated number sequences.
2. Sometimes, you're awoken in the middle of the night, and a clear voice is speaking within you that isn't your usual mental voice.
3. You have an inner knowing that your guide is present.
4. You experience interesting phenomena like books falling off shelves for no reason.
5. You come across the same message multiple times from various unconnected sources.
6. The area between your eyebrows tingles and pulses. This is your third eye or ajna chakra.
7. You're receiving more and more unique ideas.
8. Your dreams become more vivid, last longer, and appear to have a real-time feeling rather than the illogical shift from one scene to the next typical of dreams.
9. You get the sense that you're not alone — not figuratively, but literally.
10. You feel physical sensations like touch, inexplicable and illogical shifts in temperature, etc.
11. You get a tingling sensation at the back of your neck, toward the base.

If you'd like to be confident that you genuinely are establishing contact with your guides, you'll find it beneficial to journal every extraordinary experience. You should ensure you're being truly guided and not merely assuming your interpretation of a situation is from your spirit guides. The best way to be certain is through constant observation. Become a scientist, noting everything you receive and comparing and contrasting events.

Do not share what you're up to with people who will likely look at you as if you're doing "woo-woo stuff" because they'll probably think you're crazy. You may presume they're right when they aren't. You can let others know later (only if you're inspired to) when you've developed trust and have connected with your guides often enough to be convinced they're real. You can't be shaken at that point because you have proof of your experiences to back up your claim. You now trust your intuition.

Skeptics will belittle your conviction by referring to your lived experiences as "anecdotal evidence only," but don't let that bother you. Think of it like trying to explain to someone from the Stone Age that a small little device held in the palm of your hand can help you pinpoint exactly where you are on Earth or watch silly cat videos. They'd find it hard to believe if they didn't see it themselves!

In the meantime, journaling will help you track the patterns and understand when your guides are present. Also, it is an excellent tool for keeping your mind focused on establishing contact. Another thing you should do is check in with those who understand the reality of spirit guides so they can offer helpful pointers.

Chapter 7: Cultivating Deeper Bonds

Some people are satisfied with surface-level manifestations of spiritual matters. They are content with seeing license plate numbers and digital displays with synchronistic or "angel" numbers, but they aren't too keen on seeing how deep the rabbit hole goes. The fact that you're reading this book implies you want more for yourself than that. This is commendable because many benefits are had from developing a deeper connection with your spirit guides. By strengthening and deepening your bond with these beings, you will experience transformation for the better across every aspect of your life.

Deepen your bond with your spirit guides.
https://pixabay.com/photos/magical-woman-fantasy-creative-6046020/

The Core Essence of Developing a Deeper Connection

What's the whole point of wanting to deepen your connection with your spirit guides? Well, the business of life is not easy to navigate, so it certainly helps to have access to your inner wisdom on command. The deeper your connection with your spiritual side, the easier it is to connect with your guides, who will offer profound information that could only be classified as wisdom. They'll communicate using dreams, synchronicity, intuition, and other means necessary. Many people wake up each day feeling lost and confused. They live their lives in a haze. They have no idea what they want to do. However, as a person with a deep bond with your spirit guides, you will never have to deal with the torture of confusion. You will be aware of your true purpose in life because you have access to unparalleled guidance.

The ultimate goal of developing a powerful tie with your spirit guides is to help you embrace the Divine Feminine energy. They'll offer guidance to help you break the shackles of limiting beliefs and perspectives that have made it impossible to allow the Divine Mother's love and light to flow through your life. Your spirit guides can help you develop a broader perspective, showing you how many more choices you have than you previously assumed. For instance, if you're struggling in your relationships, they'll show you how to love yourself. Once you do, you'll realize you never had to struggle or beg to be loved, and the right love will come your way through more paths than one. Or have you always assumed there's only one way to earn a living? Your guides can open your eyes to show you unlimited potential, revealing opportunities for abundance you may have overlooked all this time. They will show you how to access the Divine Mother's benevolence.

Saved By Her Guide

Kachi had been planning a trip to Spain for a long time. She dreamed of visiting the country for her whole life and fantasized about walking down the beautiful Paleo de la Castellana and the Calle de Preciados. When she'd finally saved enough money and could take her vacation, she was beyond ecstatic. So, imagine what she must have felt like when she had the dream the night before. Her guide, who she was used to meeting in dreams, had shown up.

Wordlessly, he took her hand, and the scene became the airport. They were standing on the asphalt, watching a plane take flight. The scene shifted again. This time, Kachi and her guide were in the clouds above the plane. They watched as it crashed.

Then, Kachi was awake, but her eyes were still shut. On her bed, she felt her hand being urgently squeezed. It was the same hand the guide held in her dreams. She got the message, "Don't go." Kachi was miffed, but she wasn't about to disobey her guide. She tried to call the airline to warn them about the imminent crash, but no one took her seriously. After all, people played pranks like this all the time, and if the airline kept grounding planes, they'd soon be out of business. There was nothing further she could do. That night, she watched the news coverage of the plane crash her guide saved her from. This is just one of many ways your guide can help you.

A Financial Turnaround

Jeremy was a simple person who never believed in spiritual concepts. As a man who had to work multiple jobs to survive, he did the best he could, but he felt that his life lacked meaning. A series of events would eventually lead him to discover that spirit guides are real. So, he took a leap of faith to contact his spirit guide.

From that point forward, Jeremy began to find reasons to get out of bed in the morning other than to survive. He was more than happy to explore the teachings his guides offered him, and he could see how his emotional well-being improved. However, he wanted his financial life to improve, and so he brought the matter forward in meditation.

Jeremy knew next to nothing about finances or how to manage money, so rather than be specific about how he wanted help, he simply told his guides to help him in whatever ways they felt best. His social media was constantly flooded with messages about how to be your own boss, but he never believed he was cut out for that.

Three days after Jeremy set his intention for financial success, he was fired from two of his jobs. The week after, the remaining business he worked for shut down because the owners declared bankruptcy. Jeremy was confused. After all, he had asked his guides for assistance with his finances. Instead, he had lost all earning power. Downcast, he revisited the matter with his guides in a meditation session. He received one word in response to his query, "Trust."

Moments later, his friend Michaela knocked on his door. As they spoke, Michaela mentioned she was taking a class on trading cryptocurrency. Having watched too many YouTube videos on cryptocurrency scams, trading them was the last thing Jeremy thought to give his attention. Yet there was a palpable electricity in the air as soon as the words left Michaela's mouth. For Jeremy, time stood still. Once more, he got the message internally, "Trust."

Fast forward a few months later, and Jeremy is doing phenomenally well as a cryptocurrency trader, making his monthly salary in a matter of weeks and compounding his profits. If his guides hadn't gotten him out of his job, he wouldn't have had the time or focus to learn this new skill that did more than pay the bills and let him survive.

Setting Time Aside for Spirit

If you want to get better at something, you need to practice consistently. Set aside time each day to engage in your spiritual practices to help you get a stronger connection with your guides. How can you pull this off?

1. Before arbitrarily picking a time, try different times of the day. Some people feel much better when they practice first thing in the morning, others last thing at night, and others may prefer the middle of their day. It all comes down to your schedule and where you can find room for your guides. If you have the time, you could carve out at least 10 minutes thrice a day for your practice, but if you don't, 10 to 15 minutes once a day at the same time is optimum.

2. If you're unaccustomed to meditating or focusing on something for a while, you should start with shorter durations. Once more, 10 to 15 minutes is a good starting point. As you progress, you may naturally notice you're giving more and more time than usual to your practice. If you have a hard time lasting longer, work your way up from 15 minutes to 20 minutes gradually. When you become comfortable focusing for 20 minutes on your spiritual practice, you can ramp it up to 25 minutes. Keep adding five minutes each time you notice you can sit still without being as distracted as you used to be.

3. Think of your spiritual practices, like brushing your teeth. They're not optional or negotiable. Your decision has nothing to do with your feelings. You will still clean your teeth whether or

not you see gunk on them or if you're happy or sad. Use the same approach in your spiritual life. With this mindset, you will never be tempted to skip a day. You'll do what you should, regardless of whether you feel in the mood or not.

4. Working with more than one tool to connect with your guides? Get organized by assigning a set time to each practice. Note that there may be certain times when your guides have so much to do with you. At times like these, you should allow flexibility so that you do not interrupt the process. When that's not the case, work with your set schedule.

Personalizing Your Rituals

You could look up already-established rituals people use to connect with your spirit guides. However, it would be of greater benefit to create your own. Crafting your own ritual means working with your intuition, which is one way your guides communicate with you. Since they know you better than anyone else, they will know what elements to include and what actions you need to perform to establish a greater connection between you than if you went with someone else's methods. The process will give you a sense of empowerment because it will convince you that you can communicate with your spirit directly without an intermediary's help. So, now you understand the necessity for personalizing your rituals. Here are five ideas to help you with the process:

1. Consider making offerings to your guides at the start of your rituals to demonstrate your gratitude.
2. Add nature to your practices when and where possible. You could work with specific plants and stones, representations of animals, and elements like sunlight, moonlight, rainwater, etc.
3. You can work your rituals into your breakfast, lunch, or dinner. Think of it like having a meal with your guides.
4. If you're a music lover, incorporating music into your rituals is an excellent way to deepen your experience. You could chant, hum, or play ambient music that puts you in the mood.
5. Incense is another excellent addition to help you banish unwanted or stale energy in your spiritual space and amplify your guide's energy.

6. Make the lighting in your ritual space softer, and you'll connect with your guides more easily.

Alternative Modalities for Connecting with Your Guides

Oracle Cards: These cards have lovely pictures and words printed on them. You can work with them to get more clarity on what your guides are communicating to you. When you have your decks ready, begin by thanking your guides and letting them know what you'd like guidance on and that you want clear messages that are impossible to misunderstand. Then, shuffle the cards while you ask the question.

Oracle cards can help you get more clarity on what your guides are communicating to you.
https://unsplash.com/photos/the-big-bang-theory-dvd-Lh3cimWevas?utm_content=creditShareLink&utm_medium=referral&utm_source=unsplash

When your intuition leads you to stop shuffling, pull out a card. These cards often come with interpretations so you can get a general idea of the answer you're receiving. Then, sit in silence to see what else your guides will share to offer further clarity.

If you don't get anything extra but still need reassurance, state the intention while shuffling the cards once more, stop shuffling when you're led to, and pull out another card. This card will clarify your answer. When you're done, you can write the insights you received in your journal to review later.

Dreamwork: This modality is excellent for getting clarity, confirmation, healing, miracles, and more from your guides. How does it work? Firstly, before you go to bed, you have to set your intention that you would like to connect with your guide in your dream. You can state this intention aloud or say it in your mind. A simple sentence will suffice.

You need a journal dedicated to recording your dreams and their interpretations. If you're accustomed to waking up during the night, you should always bring your intention to mind rather than hurry to open your eyes or roll out of bed. Dreamwork is impossible without good dream recall. How can you get better at remembering your dreams?

1. When you wake up from a dream, whatever you do, don't open your eyes and don't move your body. If you do, the odds are high that you will forget your dreams.

2. When you go to bed, practice recalling everything you did that day by starting with the last thing you did before getting into bed. In the beginning, this won't be easy to accomplish, but with time and practice, you'll get better.

3. When you have dreams, you use the same method of recalling the last thing you saw or felt when you were in the dream, then moving backward from there. You may lose all recollection if you attempt to remember the first thing you dreamt.

4. Take reality checks throughout your day. For instance, you could look at a clock, look away, and then look at it again. If you notice the time is still the same, you're definitely not dreaming. In dreams, the time tends to waver. The same can be said for all written text. Another excellent check is to bounce your feet against the floor and see if you hover or fly. Also, ask yourself what you were doing before, whatever you're doing now, and keep working your way backward. This works because if you do it in a dream, you'll catch on that there's something odd about going from your living room to the Eiffel Tower when you actually live in New Jersey. The more you perform these reality checks, the more likely those habits will spill over into your dreams. When you do the checks and realize you're dreaming, you can become lucid and ask your guide to come to you.

Automatic Writing: When you practice automatic writing, you're not thinking about the words coming through. You simply allow them to flow from the pen onto the paper, trusting that the messages come directly from your spirit guides. You first need to set an intention about what you want guidance on. Next, get into a meditative state. When you arrive at the point where your mind and body are still and in the moment, you may write. Don't overthink what comes out of you. Don't try to edit it. If it is gibberish, allow it. As you continue, your words will eventually take on meaning and offer you a profound perspective on whatever you want to know. When you're done, thank your guides for coming through and reviewing what you've received so you can internalize it.

Chapter 8: Meditative Pathways: Accessing Higher Consciousness

There is no better way to attain higher consciousness than through meditation. Far too many people are stuck worrying about the future or regretting their past to focus on the present. Remaining in the here and now is a prerequisite for attaining higher consciousness. In this chapter, you'll learn everything about the different forms of meditation and how to use them to access this higher consciousness, which will positively affect your life.

Mediation leads to a higher state of consciousness.
https://pixabay.com/photos/meditate-woman-yoga-zen-meditating-1851165/

What Is Higher Consciousness?

Higher consciousness is a concept covering multiple principles. The first thing you need to understand about the state of consciousness is that it sets you free from the idea of limitation and lack. As Bashar (channeled by Darryl Anka) once said, there is no such thing as lack — only an abundance of lack because abundance is all there is. This may sound like gibberish and "copium" to those who haven't woken up yet. However, there is truth to that statement. By developing your connection to higher consciousness and keeping it open, you will experience this truth in real-time. Nothing gives you peace of mind quite like the understanding that higher consciousness offers you.

Higher consciousness is about an expanded state of awareness. It is about perceiving things outside the purview of the physical world or anything your five senses can distinguish. When you operate from a state of higher consciousness, you realize that attempting to fix your life through action alone is like looking at your reflection in a mirror and manipulating its lips with your fingers, hoping it'll smile. Higher consciousness is understanding that all things come from awareness of being first. In other words, if you want that reflection to smile, you're going to have to smile, and only then will you see what you want to see. Higher consciousness is about being, not doing. Whatever you want to accomplish or become, you must first be it. How do you pull this off?

First, you must accept that the version of you who has accomplished what you want already exists as you. Then, assume you are that person and operate from that perspective. As someone who's in touch with a higher consciousness, you are a self-aware person who understands how you feel, why you feel the way you do, how those feelings affect your thoughts, and how they come together to motivate you to take action. You understand the interrelationship between thoughts, emotions, and actions.

It is impossible to be in this heightened sense of awareness without having a sense of empathy and acting on it compassionately. You do not see any distinction between yourself and the next person from this state. Jesus was explaining this to his disciples by saying that as they helped others around them, they were really helping him. Higher consciousness is knowing that you and the others are the same. This knowledge does wonders for your creativity and intuition because you'll find it easy to tap into the "spiritual internet" and draw from the collective conscious or unconscious whatever new ideas you seek to create, understand, heal, grow, or make other intentions real.

Benefits of Accessing Higher Consciousness

Peace of Mind: One of the greatest gifts of higher consciousness is that it keeps you in the present moment. In other words, if you are a very anxious person, constantly worried and depressed, embodying the higher consciousness ideal of being here and now will sort out your issues, giving you what is described as "the peace that passes all understanding."

A Broader Range of Perception: Your connection with higher consciousness means you can pick up on information inaccessible to most because they do not operate through any other modality than the physical. They rely too heavily on what their five senses tell them. Did you know that sunlight gets to you 500 seconds late? Did you also know that what is observed depends on the observer's state of mind? This begs the question, what is the ultimate reality?

The answer is there is an infinite number of possibilities. It's a matter of choosing which of these possibilities you prefer. For instance, if you'd like to become financially successful, it doesn't matter that you've never experienced this as an objective physical reality. It also doesn't matter that your current reality does not match what you'd prefer. By remaining in the state of higher consciousness, you manifest your desired ideal by assuming you are already a financially successful person. Then, the physical world — a delayed mirror of your assumptions about who you are until the point of changing them — will have to show you evidence of your new state of consciousness or being in due time.

Stronger Intuition: Some people only ever receive intuitive messages when in extreme need or danger. What if you could remain in constant contact with your intuition at every point in time? This is an essential benefit that accessing higher consciousness offers you. Think of it like having an eye in the sky, helping you bypass obstacles and threats, and leading you through the shortest and best paths to wherever you want.

In truth, the benefits of accessing higher consciousness are endless. Your life will once more be flooded with meaning and purpose so that you look forward to each new day. You'll develop a stronger backbone, able to handle whatever life throws at you because you understand that all roads lead to your greatest good. You'll have better problem-solving skills on account of how much more creative you are thanks to this infinite well of creativity that is higher consciousness.

What's more, the relationship between you and yourself will take a turn for the better, helping you realize your power, value, and worth. Your relationships with others will also become richer, with every moment offering up a new, more amazing gift than the last as you commune with the people in your life.

Meditation

Meditation is about so much more than trying to relax or destress. These days, clear capitalism has sunk its talons once more into something originally meant to help humanity. Look it up, and you'll find someone's trying to sell you an app, scented candles, a subscription course, or something else often packaged in a way that strips the essence from the concept to make it easier to sell. After all, it's easier to market speed and ease, a silver bullet, a quick fix.

Meditation is a practice requiring commitment and the willingness to maintain focused awareness. You do it on your own while sitting or reclining in a semi-upright position. Group meditations are also possible, but in connecting with your Divine Feminine, you should meditate on your own to learn to focus on a single thing without getting distracted.

Meditation isn't just something you do when you feel you need to unwind. Sure, it works for that purpose. But if you want to go beyond focused attention and deep relaxation to an altered state of consciousness where you perceive the reality that it powers, you can do so with meditation. It's a tool that leads to greater mindfulness. You can use it as a gateway to the many worlds within you and to connect directly to higher consciousness.

Even science has caught on that there's much more to meditation than sitting in silence and accomplishing nothing. A study by the University of the Sunshine Coast revealed that you develop better attention with mindfulness. The researchers worked with 81 participants at least 60 years old, getting them involved in mindfulness, and they were examined six months later. The meditators had improved immensely at keeping their attention on one thing from the changes in their brain structure resulting from their eight-week practice. They also found that people who meditate or use other mindfulness practices get better at processing information through their five senses as their perception becomes sharper. Some findings clearly demonstrate that mindfulness makes the brain more malleable and open to changing and developing for the better, as meditation causes neuroplasticity.

Types of Meditation

You can choose from a plethora of meditation techniques, depending on your goals. Some are dynamic, meaning you have to walk or move to do them. There's no such thing as one form of meditation being superior to others. It's best to try them and keep doing what resonates with you the best. Some meditations require keeping your attention on a specific thing throughout, like a candle's flame, a spot on the wall, the sound of dripping water, a smell, your breath, a mantra, etc. With time, you'll sustain your attention without getting distracted, and when you lose track, you're quick to return your attention to the object you're focusing on.

There's open monitoring meditation, where you allow your attention to wander while remaining detached from what you perceive on the inside or the outside. You don't judge anything but perceive all things as they are. You remain non-reactive. Then there's effortless presence, where your attention isn't on any specific thing. Your only focus is on being here now. Arguably, you could think of this meditation as the ultimate meditation, getting to the point of silence and formlessness where you're everything and nothing. That sentence will make more sense as you practice. With these general groupings in mind, here are specific techniques you could try:

Zen Meditation: Sit on the floor using a cushion or a mat with your legs crossed in lotus or half lotus. You can sit on a chair. Just ensure your spine is straight. You remain focused on your breath as it goes in and out through your nostrils, counting your breath and starting the count over when you're distracted. Alternatively, you can simply sit, be here now, and observe what's popping up in your mind and what's happening in your environment without overthinking anything.

Vipassana: First, you have to learn to concentrate, which comes from basic meditation, where you notice your breath, whether it's the feeling of air flowing through your nostrils or the rise and fall of your stomach. This is your primary focus. Stick with it, and other things will arise for you to notice, whether in your body or via thought. When you feel this new element has taken your attention away from your primary focus, give it a moment more, and label it in your mind with a suitable word that describes it, like "smelling," "desiring," "thinking," "remembering," etc. It should be a general word. There's no need for detailed labeling. Rather than label a sound "airplane," "TV," or "laughter," choose "hearing." Rather than "headache," "cramps," or "pins and needs," use "sensation." In place of anger, joy, confusion, etc., "feeling" will do. When you label the thing, turn your attention back to the primary focus.

Mantra Meditation: A mantra is a sound that may or may not have meaning. It could be a word or a series of words. To perform the mantra meditation, sit in silence and begin chanting it by repeating it aloud or in your mind. If you do it aloud, you'll notice subtle vibrations moving through you. There may be times when you don't want to chant aloud, then do so in your mind. Here are some of the most common mantras:

- Om
- Yam
- Ham
- So, ham
- Rama
- Om namah Shivaya
- Om Shanti
- Om mani padme hum
- Hu
- Brzee

You can repeat your chosen mantra 108 times or 1008 – or set a timer and keep chanting until it goes off!

Practical Tips for Effective, Regular Meditation

1. Always set an intention for your meditation before you begin. If you want to relax, set that intention. If you want to go further, lock that in your mind first.
2. You should always meditate somewhere free from distractions, especially when you're just starting. After a while, you'll find you can meditate even in the middle of a busy, noisy street or on the dancefloor in a nightclub — if there's ever a reason you have to meditate in those places.
3. Select a meditation method you resonate with. If something doesn't work for you, move on to something else.

4. Your meditation experience will be deeper if you take the time to set up the ambiance and make your space sacred. Soft lighting, candlelight, incense, and natural elements are excellent ways to make your space more sacred.

The Challenges and Rewards of Living with Higher Consciousness

It would be remiss of this book not to enlighten you of the challenges you will face when you choose to live a life full of higher consciousness. You'll become more aware of sensations, receiving extra information from sources other than your five physical ones. This may be overwhelming for the beginner who is only becoming deliberate about pursuing their spiritual growth. If you ever feel this way, you'll find it helpful to ground yourself in reality. Take a walk in nature, or spend time in it. If you can walk barefoot on natural ground, do that. You could practice scanning your body, working from your feet up to your head, and being aware of how the muscles feel in each part. Also, be firm with your boundaries because your practice may draw individuals who want to take advantage of your fresh energy.

Additionally, sometimes it will feel like you're taking a step forward only to take several backward because you're coming up against the roots of the patterns you've unconsciously executed without thought. You'll come face to face with your ego, which doesn't want you to continue on this path because it fears you'll see it for what it is: an illusion, and it will die. The fix here is to be compassionate toward yourself as you deal with the internal push and pull. Accept that this feeling is part of the dance of spiritual evolution.

Spiritual evolution can be a lonely journey, as not many people are prepared to deprogram themselves as you're doing. You may lose old friends and experience distance between you and your family. Seek out people working consciously on their spiritual growth, just like you, so you don't feel alone and will be encouraged to continue being your authentic self.

The rewards of living a life of higher consciousness far outweigh whatever downsides you may imagine. Nothing in the world could offer you the amount of inner peace that this modality of life can. The sands of time and space may shift under your feet, but you're not shaken because higher consciousness is the ultimate foundation of all life, so you know you won't fall. You can trust in its stability. You become part of those souls who are getting in touch with their compassionate, empathetic sides and sharing that warmth and love with a world in sore need of healing and peace. You become more intuitive and creative, living a life where every breath you take is pregnant with purpose and passion, a life where you realize the only things that matter are here, now, and how you occupy this space and time.

Chapter 9: Prayer as a Sacred Ritual

What Is Prayer?

Prayer is universal. It is communicating with the Divine, with that which is beyond comprehension, regardless of what you call it or how you interact with the force. It's invoking the power of the source of all life, channeling it toward achieving a goal. It's showing appreciation and, when needed, seeking intervention to change something in your life or another's for the better. Typically, people pray to their ancestors, deities, or whatever versions of God they believe in. Prayer isn't only about asking for things but also being thankful and offering praise in words and with rituals and offerings. Prayer isn't like regular communication because you're connecting with a power that is anything but physical.

Prayer is communication with the Divine.
https://pixabay.com/photos/hands-body-woman-posture-hand-5037846/

People have always prayed, whether or not they fully understand what or who they're praying to. You can pray on your own or as part of a group. For some, prayer is the performance of rituals, and for others, prayer involves singing hymns, chanting incantations, and stating personal credos. Every religion in the world practices prayer in some form. With certain ideologies, prayer is something strict, with a set of rules that must be followed to the letter. For others, there's more room for creative flow, allowing you to go with your intuition. Generally, prayer has a dual nature. How? You speak to the Divine, but also, you listen. You ask in prayer, and you receive.

Science has looked into prayer and its power, specifically to see how it can lead to healing, but as usual, its results are contradictory. On the one hand, some scientists approach their research with a bias against all things spiritual, which inevitably affects their interpretation and experience of prayer. On the other hand, charlatans like cult leaders and faux prosperity preachers have weaponized their charisma to control people unwilling to think for themselves and are susceptible to being brainwashed. These people fake miracles and more, and inevitably, once scientists set their sights on them to investigate, they walk away from their studies, even more convinced that prayer is a pointless hoax.

Prayer through the Lens of Traditions and Religions

Look into the Abrahamic religions, and you'll find that prayer has always played a significant role. God's faithful followers would communicate with him through prayer, usually spontaneously, and often on their own, in the Hebraic Bible — until things changed at the start of the book of Deuteronomy, where rules and structure for prayer were laid. In the pages of the New Testament, you'll find that the prayers were more about commanding good things to happen, like healing, deliverance from demons, resurrection, etc. The Christians of those times learned to make prayer a regular thing and to do it privately. The Lord's Prayer was an excellent example that Jesus offered the people to use.

Prayer plays a significant role in the Abrahamic religions.
Elperrofeliz345678, CC BY-SA 4.0 <https://creativecommons.org/licenses/by-sa/4.0>, via Wikimedia Commons: https://commons.wikimedia.org/wiki/File:Abrahamic_religions.png

What about Judaism? Thrice a day, you must observe your prayers — the Shacharit, Mincha, and Ma'ariv. Certain religious ceremonies have much longer prayers. Generally, the Jewish prayers have two parts: the intention (or *kavanah*) and the organized aspects (the *keva*). One of the Jews' most common prayers is the *Amidah*, "The Standing Prayer." Then there are the Kabbalists, who pray with kavanot - which are *intentions tied to their prayers,* meant to ensure a swift and effective answer in response.

The Muslims call prayer *salah,* an Arabic word referring to the prayers that must be made five times daily at set times. Every Muslim knows to pray to face the direction of Mecca's Kaaba once they hear the adhan, the "call for prayer." They often begin their prayers with praise for God and his greatness. They will read portions of the Quran during their sessions, honor God by lowering themselves to the ground in prostration or sujud, and offer more praise before wrapping up with a proclamation of peace and God's mercy on everyone.

In some parts of Africa, prayer involves rituals, dancing, chanting, music, dance, and sacrifices in honor of divine beings who bless the people benevolently for their devotion. How about Eastern religions? Mantras are commonplace in Hinduism and Buddhism. However, Buddhists do not subscribe to the idea of praying to a God or Goddess. Hinduism has a philosophical prayer and meditation on the essence of specific deities.

If you want to pray, there's one thing to always remember: Your intention matters. It's much better to make your prayer as personal as possible because it will be much more sincere and less rote than praying standard prayers (unless you pray those traditional prayers with a deep focus on their meanings).

Three Forms of Prayer

Conscious Intentional Prayer: This prayer requires you to focus your mind on attaining a specific result, your intention. You need a mental picture of the fulfillment of whatever you desire. Then, you leave it for the source of all life to handle, trusting that it will take care of it at the right time, not a moment too soon or too late, and in the best way for all concerned. Intention is the engine that drives your prayer forward until it becomes a fleshed-out result for everyone to see. It's the reason you get out of bed to pursue your dreams, smash your goals, and bring your desires to pass.

By incorporating the energy of intention into your prayers, you will be clear on what you hope to receive. It focuses your energy, making you more likely to receive what you want.

Conscious, intentional prayer requires a deliberate refocusing of your mind on your objective while you pray, holding your thoughts and emotions hostage to the end of your prayer time and disciplining them so they do not stray. What you assume and how you feel as you pray must match how you'd feel if you had the answer to your prayer already. This way, you put yourself in the best position for the Divine to help you. Your actions and choices will naturally be aligned with what you desire, and it's only a matter of time before you make your dream happen.

You can find this intentionality in the *Sankalpa* of Hinduism, a solemn vow, an intention you must make before you make your dreams happen. By being deliberate in offering your Sankalpa to the Universe, keeping your focus on the end goal already being real here and now, and staying devoted to that vision, you gather energy from every plane of existence and carve your world into the exact vision you want to see.

Conscious Awareness Prayer: Conscious awareness prayer is about remaining aware of how you're being and what you're thinking from moment to moment and ensuring it aligns with the essence of God. You have to be focused when working with this prayer. But rather than seeking outcomes, you're more interested in your inner world. What are you feeling in your body? How about emotionally? What are the thoughts at the moment? Ask yourself these questions without judging yourself. You're not making a particular request because the only thing that matters is remaining firmly rooted in the present, where your past and future are nonexistent concepts. For all you know, you might as well have suddenly appeared on Earth right now.

What's the point of this prayer? You'll become more self-aware, which automatically puts you in touch with your intuition. As your desires appear during your day, you'll naturally be led toward the answers you seek. Thanks to your deeper connection with your intuition, you'll be directed to take the right actions, say the right things, and be at the right place at the right time. Conscious awareness prayer is about staying open, accepting whatever is and whatever comes afterward. One thing you'll notice with this form of worship is that it's almost like meditation, in the sense that the ongoing monologue in your head is forced to shut up, giving you peace on the inside regardless of what's happening around you. You'll receive phenomenal, life-changing insights that will change your life for the better from this state. If you practice this prayer, you won't have to pray for specific things because things line up beautifully for you.

Unconscious Awareness Prayer: With this form of prayer, there's a connection between your specific intentions and awareness of your life experience in the here and now. In other words, it's the balance between conscious intention and conscious awareness. Not only do you have moments where you focus on your intention, but you ensure you're acting as someone who already has what they seek. Even when you're confronted with the evidence of the absence of your desire in the physical, you don't allow that to phase you. You continue to fix your mind on your fully fleshed-out manifestation (in your imagination) while tracking your experience of life, ensuring your mental chatter, emotions, actions, and vision match your desired reality.

Now you understand the basic mechanics of prayer- Remember, it's not just about honoring a deity because that's what you've been taught. It's a sincere act, one you do willingly. Prayer is a profound way to cultivate presence and mindfulness. The more you pray, the more you'll experience higher consciousness.

Practical Tips for Consistent, Meaningful Prayer

1. Don't use rituals if you're not comfortable. You don't need to use specific words from set prayers if they do not resonate, nor do you need to craft yours and repeat it until it loses meaning. You can simply become aware of the moment and set your intention before you begin.
2. Find a way to fit prayer into your routine to stay consistent. You could make prayer the last thing you do at night and the first thing you do before you get out of bed in the morning. You could take advantage of your lunch breaks, the moment before you enter your office building, or before you set off for home. It's up to you.
3. Don't just ask. Receive as well. How? When you are done asking, remain seated in silence and expect an answer. Note that it may not be in words. It could be a simple feeling of completion, certainty, satisfaction, ease, or something else.
4. Journal whatever you receive from prayer. This record will show you that it indeed works and help you through times when you waver in doubt.

5. Do not beat yourself up for skipping a day or two of prayer. At the same time, understand that you'll need time to establish consistency, so be kinder to yourself.

Chapter 10: A Continual Spiral of Growth

In this final chapter, you should remember that you are a part of the Divine Feminine. You are inseparable from her grace, mercy, and love. You carry her power and essence within you.

You are a part of the Divine Feminine.
https://pixabay.com/photos/horoscope-fate-goddess-space-7650723/

Celebrating Your Inner Goddess

As you develop your relationship with the Divine Feminine, you need to celebrate yourself. You must acknowledge how far you've come because it's no mean feat that you decided to pursue this path and followed through on your decision even though the world is a place where the toxic masculine attempts to smother the Divine Feminine in everyone. You have chosen the path less trodden, and as a result, you've become one of many who will eventually help the world break free from the imbalance of energies it's currently suffering.

Embracing your inner Goddess is not easy because it means overcoming the tendencies you've instilled in you since birth. It is a course of action that requires unlearning, and it is brutal. You have to chip away at the things you once thought of as part of your original self, realizing that they're simply ideas from others you accepted as your identity. There are times on this journey when it feels so painful and downright impossible to progress. So, if you've chosen to persevere and push through, you should definitely celebrate the courage and progress you've made so far.

It isn't easy to convince yourself that there are better ways than working yourself to the bone to accomplish abundance. Like others in the past, your default response to the idea of not needing to work hard to accomplish abundance would have been to scoff and laugh at its seeming ridiculousness. However, you have dared to prove this truth to yourself, which is not easy in the face of the very persistent illusion of needing to work yourself into the ground before accomplishing abundance.

There may have been times when life appeared to mock you. There may have been moments when you wondered if you weren't being silly or ridiculous, trying out this "Divine Feminine thing," wondering if it wouldn't be better to return to the status quo you were used to and familiar with. However, you've somehow found the courage to keep going. Your willingness, perseverance, and faith have rewarded you with evidence of new, better ways to achieve your dreams in life. It is something worth celebrating.

As you continue incorporating the Divine Feminine energy into your life, recognize that you will not always maintain a fixed level of this energy. You are not a static being. No one is. Everyone is designed to continue evolving, to fluctuate with respect to the dynamics of the Divine pendulum swinging from one energy to another. Therefore, if you find yourself out of balance, the last thing you should do is beat yourself up. Instead, be glad that you now have the consciousness to be aware of this shift in balance and do what you must return to your center.

It serves no one to feel terrible about being imperfect or flawed. The very nature of imperfection is a perfect design in nature. It is a feature, not a flaw, so don't dwell on your mistakes. See yourself as a work of art constantly, eternally in progress, ever evolving into something more refined. This way, rather than harshly criticize yourself, you can celebrate how far you've come from who you used to be to who you are now. You'll be excited about the prospect of who you'll morph into along your journey of embracing the Divine Feminine within.

Nurture Your

Your intuition will guide you further along the path to meeting your most balanced self.
Photo by Edz Norton on Unsplash https://unsplash.com/photos/text-j5itydU55FI

One of the most essential things to recall is constantly staying in touch with your intuition. It is your intuition that will guide you further and further along the path to meeting your most balanced self. Your intuition is that soft, still voice that will let you know when you're deviating from your goals. Whatever you do, honor it without question. At this point, you should have discovered the futility of attempting to interpret intuition using logic and rationality. It is much better to embrace it without question and discover later why it was essential to heed that voice warning and steering you this way and that.

Your ego seduces you into returning to the trap of logic. Remember, the idea behind logic is rooted in that which is familiar and already known. How can you possibly grow if you remain in the spaces you already know? How could you discover new lands if you only stay at home? How do you become more than you are if you insist on remaining exactly as you are? Yet logic insists that you keep everything the same. Logic is ego-driven because your ego fears that if you dare to explore the unfamiliar, you may put yourself at risk, and it will no longer exist. The one thing the ego fears above everything else is nonexistence. So, it's essential to break away from the habits of the ego, to shun the tendency to retreat into the safety of logic and reason, and instead realize your existence can't be permanently extinguished or erased. Why? Because you are a soul, first and foremost, before a human being. You are an eternal being, one that can't be destroyed.

You may look around and see disease and death claiming people's lives. However, rest assured that those souls continue their next adventure in another reincarnation. Right now, you are a soul having a human adventure. Your ego doesn't understand it because it's terrified that this is all there is to life. It continues to do what it must to shield you. In its misguided opinion, it is keeping you safe from harm.

If there's one thing your ego knows about your intuition, it's that it will lead you into depths that it cannot fathom, where it suspects it will be destroyed. In a sense, this is true. As you practice expressing the energy of the Divine Feminine in your life, you will naturally be connected to higher consciousness and realize that the ego is a tool you can put down and pick up as needed. You'll learn that everything connected to your ego —who you are, what you like and dislike, your name, how much you make, what you do, etc. — is nothing but a mask or a costume. It's like putting on clothes and assuming they are who you are instead of knowing you can take them off your body and put on different ones. You can burn the clothes and still be perfectly fine.

So, if you are ever led to participate in a random conversation, even though it's not in your nature to interrupt others when speaking, you should. If you're not an avid reader but suddenly have the urge to read a specific book, listen to your intuition. If you've gone your entire life hating the idea of mathematics and numbers and yet suddenly want to learn about business bookkeeping or accounting, listen to your gut and follow through. If you've always assumed that you could never create anything close to the beautiful works of art you have seen from painters, sculptors, and other artists, but you suddenly are bitten by the art bug, follow that impulse and see where it goes.

In other words, be like a child. Have you ever watched little children when they play? If you take a toy away from them, they immediately pivot to the next shiny, interesting object. They don't pause to consider whether they want to play with that thing or not. They simply follow their little hearts. Unfortunately, over time, society dulls the instinct to follow your intuition and emphasizes the need to exercise caution and be logical, rational, and restrained in affairs of the heart.

Well, dear reader, it is time for you to throw that book out. It is time to return to being your inner child. Allow your intuition to lead you. Trust that it will always take you to beautiful places and watch the magic unfolding in your life. If you genuinely want to walk the path of the Divine Feminine, you don't have a choice in this matter, for it is through your intuition that her energy and wisdom flow and express themselves in your life. Through your intuition, your spirit guides will lead you where you must go to experience the next best version of yourself. By following your intuition, you offer a gift to others, showing them the path to healing and reflecting on the possibilities they could enjoy.

Conclusion

You can no longer afford to play small. You can't afford to keep doing things the way you've always have. Having read this book, you've answered the Divine Feminine's call, and now her fire rages within you, demanding attention. Should you choose to disregard the information you've learned from these pages, you'll find that the costumes and masks you continue to insist on wearing will become heavier than ever. Trust this one fact: You do not want the heaviness to progress past a certain point. The burden of answering the Divine Feminine's call is much lighter than insisting on maintaining the charade of the life you've lived so far. She's offering you something far better than you can imagine. There's only one way to receive it: to dare to step into the unknown.

It is time to burn the bridge that still connects you to all that you hold familiar and dear. It's time to step into new territory to discover what more lies within you. You carry greatness, strength, resilience, courage, love, light, abundance, and many other gifts only you can discover by daring to take the Divine Feminine's hand. Allow her to show you the way to your authentic self. You deserve to live the life you've always dreamed of. For the longest time, you've always suspected that things could be better than they are, and you are right. You now know how to achieve this better life you've always wanted. It would be a crying shame if you denied yourself the gift of fulfilling your dreams.

Do you feel terrified? Are you being dogged by uncertainty and fear? This is perfectly normal. It is to be expected. However, you must demonstrate courage. It does not mean you will not be afraid. It means you will acknowledge your fear and still act despite it. It is a sad state of affairs that society has taught everyone to be afraid of being afraid. There is a reason for this and it is an insidious one. Here's a good rule of thumb for you to live by going forward: If something terrifies you or makes you afraid, that is exactly what you should chase after. Your fears give you clues about what you should be doing with your life. So, if the thought of embracing the Divine Feminine and finding your inner Goddess terrifies you, you know what to do. It is your one task; you must see it through to the end and beyond. The fear you feel may tell you that you aren't ready. But that is a big lie.

Remember, there are no coincidences. There's only one reason you and this book have found each other: you are ready *now*. You're as prepared as you'll ever be. So, take the plunge and see what's on the other side. Beware, though, you will never be the same again, but it'll be for the better.

You're never alone. Remember that. You are the Divine Mother's own.

Here's another book by Mari Silva that you might like

Your Free Gift
(only available for a limited time)

Thanks for getting this book! If you want to learn more about various spirituality topics, then join Mari Silva's community and get a free guided meditation MP3 for awakening your third eye. This guided meditation mp3 is designed to open and strengthen ones third eye so you can experience a higher state of consciousness. Simply visit the link below the image to get started.

https://spiritualityspot.com/meditation

Or, Scan the QR code!

References

Azman, T. (2023, October 16). Spirit Guides: How They Can Offer Comfort and Guidance When You Need It Most. Mindvalley Blog. https://blog.mindvalley.com/spirit-guides/#h-what-is-a-spirit-guide-and-how-do-they-touch-your-life

Budson, A. E. (2021, May 13). Can Mindfulness Change Your Brain? Harvard Health. https://www.health.harvard.edu/blog/can-mindfulness-change-your-brain-202105132455

Chang, P. (2017, September 9). Why The Imbalance of the Divine Feminine & Divine Masculine Energies Is The Root Cause Of Human Suffering. Conscious Reminder. https://consciousreminder.com/2017/09/09/imbalance-divine-feminine-divine-masculine-energies-root-cause-human-suffering/

Dienstmann, G. (2019, July 13). Types of Meditation - An Overview of 23 Meditation Techniques. Live and Dare; Live and Dare. https://liveanddare.com/types-of-meditation/

Isbel, B., Weber, J., Lagopoulos, J., Stefanidis, K., Anderson, H., & Summers, M. J. (2020). Neural Changes in Early Visual Processing after 6 Months of Mindfulness Training in Older Adults. Scientific Reports, 10(1). https://doi.org/10.1038/s41598-020-78343-w

Humphreys, L. C. (2021, October 28). Duality. God Is Both Masculine and Feminine. Medium. https://medium.com/@laurenhumphreys737/duality-god-is-both-masculine-and-feminine-d45b1e3d31e5

Lee, K. A. (2015, May 25). The 4 Female Archetypes of the Moon (+ How to Work with Them). The Moon School. https://www.themoonschool.org/archetypes/four-female-archetypes/

Louise, R. (2014). Loving the Divine Feminine, Integrating the Whole. Elephant Journal. https://www.elephantjournal.com/2014/06/loving-the-divine-feminine-integrating-the-whole/

Lutz, A., Davidson, R. J., & Ricard, M. (2014). Neuroscience Reveals the Secrets of Meditation's Benefits. Scientific American. https://www.scientificamerican.com/article/neuroscience-reveals-the-secrets-of-meditation-s-benefits/

Sage, M. (2023). The Universal Power of Prayer. Psychic Bloggers. https://psychicbloggers.com/archives/21634

Sears, K. (2020). The Basics of 7 Feminine Archetypes from Jungian Psychology. Kaitlyn Sears Yoga. https://kaitlynsearsyoga.com/blogs/news/7-feminine-archetypes

The World Thinks. (2024). Awaken Your Inner Goddess: Discovering the Strength and Beauty Within. The World Thinks. https://theworldthinks.com/awaken-your-inner-goddess/

Tiodar, A. (2021). 11 Qualities of the Divine Feminine Explained. Subconscious Servant. https://subconsciousservant.com/divine-feminine-qualities/

Tiodar, A. (2021, July 14). Divine Masculine: 11 Key Qualities Explained. Subconscious Servant. https://subconsciousservant.com/divine-masculine/

Yugay, I. (2022). 15 Ways to Balance Masculine and Feminine Energy for Resilience. Mindvalley Blog. https://blog.mindvalley.com/masculine-feminine-energy/

Young, A. (2022). 11 Signs Your Spirit Guides Are Communicating with You. Subconscious Servant. https://subconsciousservant.com/signs-your-spirit-guides-are-trying-to-communicate/

Young, A. (2022). How to Find, Connect & Communicate with Your Spirit Guides. Subconscious Servant. https://subconsciousservant.com/how-to-find-your-spirit-guide/

www.ingramcontent.com/pod-product-compliance
Lightning Source LLC
Chambersburg PA
CBHW072152200426
43209CB00052B/1151